The Owner of the House
New Collected Poems
1940–2001

THE OWNER OF THE HOUSE
NEW COLLECTED POEMS
1940–2001

LOUIS SIMPSON

*

AMERICAN POETS CONTINUUM SERIES, NO. 78

BOA Editions, Ltd. * *Rochester, NY* * *2003*

First Edition
03 04 05 06   7 6 5 4 3 2 1

Publications by BOA Editions, Ltd.—
a not-for-profit corporation under section 501 (c) (3)
of the United States Internal Revenue Code—
are made possible with the assistance of grants from
the Literature Program of the New York State Council on the Arts,
the Literature Program of the National Endowment for the Arts,
the Sonia Raiziss Giop Charitable Foundation,
the Lannan Foundation,
as well as from the Mary S. Mulligan Charitable Trust,
the County of Monroe, NY,
Ames-Amzalak Memorial Trust,
and The CIRE Foundation.

See page 408 for special individual acknowledgments.

Cover Design: Daphne Poulin-Stofer
Cover Art by Don Resnick, courtesy of the artist.
Interior Design and Typesetting: Richard Foerster
Manufacturing: McNaughton & Gunn, Lithographers
BOA Logo: Mirko

LIBRARY OF CONGRESS CATALOGING-IN-PUBLICATION DATA

Simpson, Louis Aston Marantz, 1923–
    The owner of the house : new collected poems 1940-2001 / Louis Simpson.
      p. cm. — (American poets continuum series ; no. 78)
    ISBN 1-929918-38-0 (cloth : alk. paper); ISBN 1-929918-39-9 (pbk. : alk. paper)
    I. Title. II. Series. III. American poets continuum series ; v. 78.

PS3537.I75A6 2003
811'.54—dc21   2003045241

NATIONAL
ENDOWMENT
NYSCA   FOR THE ARTS

BOA Editions, Ltd.
Steven Huff, Publisher
H. Allen Spencer, Chair
A. Poulin, Jr., President & Founder (1976–1996)
260 East Avenue, Rochester, NY 14604
www.boaeditions.org

This book is dedicated to my friends:

Fred Morgan and Paula Deitz
David and Paulyn Church
Arlene Eager
Don and Jeanette Resnick
Serge Fauchereau

Contents

3
The Owner of the House

from THE ARRIVISTES: POEMS 1940–1949

from GOOD NEWS OF DEATH AND OTHER POEMS 1955

from A DREAM OF GOVERNORS 1959

from AT THE END OF THE OPEN ROAD 1963

from THE BEST HOUR OF THE NIGHT 1983

from IN THE ROOM WE SHARE 1990

from THERE YOU ARE 1995

NEW POEMS

*

The Long Afternoon

Behind the glass door
stands a *babushka*,
a grandmother doll.
It unscrews. There's another
inside, a size smaller,
that unscrews, and so on.

A pipe called a *hookah*
with a malachite bowl . . .

The gramophone wheezes,
scratches, and speaks:
"Say It With Music."
White flannels and knees
intently two-stepping
step out on the floor.

At four there's a breeze.
The bamboo trunks creak
and talk in the lane.
A house lizard hops
from the vine to the rail . . .
cocks his head at me.

"Remember?" he croaks.
Dear brother, I do!

Nero in Love

G. L. B. Wiehen,
W pronounced as V,
was a quiet, soft-spoken man.
He taught French and played the organ.

We were reading *Britannicus*
with Mister Wiehen, and came to the place
where Nero tells how he saw Junie.
He was filled with a "curious desire"
to see her when she was conveyed
in the night, secretly, to the palace . . .

"Sad, her eyes shining with tears, and bright
Even in the glare of arms and torchlight,
Just as she appeared when suddenly torn
From sleep, a beauty nothing could adorn . . .
What do you expect? Disheveled innocence,
The shadows, the flames, the cries, the silence . . ."

That night, waked by the moon,
I walked through a long corridor
to a great hall, and stood like Nero
behind a pillar and gazed at Junie.
I would have done anything for her.
I would have been one of the Caesars
people prayed to, or a great poet
like Racine.

But it was not to be.
Junie became a vestal virgin.
Enraged, I plunged headlong
into a life of crime.

A Letter from Brazil

An old friend from schooldays
wrote that he was working
in Brazil, air-shipping freight.
I was in a bad patch in my life
and of no mind to answer letters.
When I did, finally, it came back
scrawled, "Address unknown."

What is it like, air-shipping freight?
If you're successful, I suppose
you can have a fine social life.
But not with "Address unknown."
I visualized a dingy room
in a street where drumming and yelling
kept you awake. You turned on the light,
and read a magazine. Opportunities
in rapidly expanding . . . Caracas.

You strapped on your money,
put your things in a suitcase,
and took the first plane out.

*

We used to walk up and down
on the barbecue, discussing
"If Dempsey had fought Tunney again."
Or if "The Flying Scotsman" raced
"The Royal Scot," which would have won?

His letter came when I had my hands full,
simultaneously being divorced
and trying to fix up the house.

And the workmen after a while
just sat down and did nothing.
This went on for days.
I had given the contractor,
like a fool, three thousand dollars
in advance. I liked the man . . .
we had intelligent conversations.
He used the money to pay his debts,
and the workmen weren't paid,
and they packed up their tools,
leaving me with a house that looked
like an egg with the shell smashed.

I had to borrow from the bank.
This time I hired a contractor
who was with an old established firm.
He came, he looked at the mess,
and said nothing, just shook his head
gently, from side to side,
called in a crew, and finished the job.

*

At the beginning of vacations
those of us who lived in Kingston
would share a car going home.
You drove over the mountains
to Mandeville, then over the hills,
and out on the Spanish Town road,
doing sixty. There's the clock
at Halfway Tree. And the town,
where you drop off, one by one,
promising to get in touch.

But this isn't true. The friends
you see during the vacation
are different from your friends at school.

The first day at home
you go for a ride on your bicycle
in the lanes. Then for a swim,
the palms dipping, the harbor
glittering, with lines of foam.

It comes back to me now
with the sound of saws and hammers.
Some beams beneath our house
have been damaged and have to be replaced.

An Old Building on Hudson Street

After Reznikoff

It was an old building
on Hudson Street, with a loft.

The elevator was just a platform
wide open on all sides.
I saw the cables and walls
going by. The operator
glanced at me and smiled.

It came to a stop
in front of an open window.
I could have stepped right out
into space!

      And this wasn't the only
open window. There were others.

Then the interview . . . The man
asked if I knew Spanish.
"Si," I said, and he nodded.
The one I would be replacing
was a *shlemiel.* Could I type?
With two fingers. Again
he nodded. I had the job!

On the day I was to start
I kept putting it off . . .
then sent a telegram saying
I could not come. That I was ill.

I kept reliving the scene.
First, the open window . . .
Then he and I were talking.

The one I would be replacing
was sweeping the floor,
coming closer, trying to hear.

The Appointment

Genaro was standing
halfway down the car.
He turned his head slowly,
the side of his head
with the hole, oozing blood.

"Thou canst not say I did it,"
I whispered.

       The man sitting next to me
gave me a look and rustled his *News*
nervously. At 14th Street he got off
with a backward glance.

          Genaro
must have got off too. He was nowhere
to be seen.

     *

There were three ahead of me.

Sports Month had an article,
"What fight would you have liked to see?"
Peter Jackson and Jim Corbett,
though you probably never heard of it,
I said to the sports writer.

Dark, dark, they all go into the dark,
the captains, merchant bankers, eminent
     men of letters, even the Silver Star.
I'd rather be a peasant, said Achilles,
on a farm, feeding pigs,
than this damned plain, in a fog.

My number was being called.
I put the magazine down.
"Can't you hear?" the man at the desk
said irritably, drest
in a little brief authority.
"You coulda missed your appointment."

So I went in. The doctor
was looking at a sheet of paper.
He glanced up and looked down again.
The doctor had gray hair,
glasses with black frames,
and hair growing out of his nose.

They like to keep you waiting.
It's a test. Still, I wasn't prepared
when Nosehair said, "Why were you talking
to yourself in the waiting room?"

I saw a shadow
sliding around the ropes
to get at me. The referee
moved it back, and then
went over and picked up the count.
"One!" The fog was clearing.

I rose to a knee,
and at "nine" to my feet.
"Was I?" I said.
"My lips may have moved a little.
I was reading a magazine."

The doctor said, "All this
about Jesus,
are you still thinking about it?"

"No," I said. "I was sick."

*

I got on at Chambers Street.
At Times Square I looked
and saw Genaro. Sitting
and pretending to read
the advertisements.

I don't give a damn, I told him.
You can all go to hell.

An Orchid

I must have been asleep
when she got out of my bed,
unpinned the orchid from her dress,
and placed it in one of my books.

A purple skeleton
staining through the pages
of the book . . . a first edition!

                *

I took her to the ballet,
and she loved it! But when
I bought tickets to Nureyev,
the best seats in the house,
she stood me up.

She was sorry—she forgot.
So she wasn't devoted
to the performing arts.

                *

It was Easter Sunday.
She was getting out of a taxi
in a hat that made people stare.

She entered, took off her shoes,
dress, stockings, everything,
until there was nothing left
but her in her Easter hat.
"Two lumps," she said, "or three?"

*

The orchid is still there,
that is, the fragments are,
paper-thin and sere . . .

the color I remember,
outline of the petals
that seemed so perfect then,
fading through the pages.

The Listeners

I walked down the street
to the harbor, by gardens
with tattered leaves and weeds,
and through an open gate.

The red roof of the house
had lost its tiles in patches,
and the windows had no glass.
A woman stood in a window

looking down. "I used to live here,"
I shouted. "Is it all right
if I just look around?"

*

A man with dreadlocks sat
on his heels, doing something
to a pot. A child stood by him.
I walked down to the shore.

A man came towards me.
His name was Rohan Moore.
Was I the owner, he asked.
No, I said, and heard

the appreciative murmur
of those who were listening
to my life as to a play.

*

Rohan Moore led the way
into the house. It was dark.

The wall was unpainted,
the railing rough to the hand.

A family lived in the room . . .
it seemed, in every corner,
and still there was a space
where a bed once stood, by the wall,

with a table, glass and spoon.
My father, looking small,
spoke again the last few words.

*

People were gathering
from every part of the house,
a dozen where four used to be.
They stood and stared silently.

I shook the hand of my guide,
now my friend. And another's.
"You can come and live here,
if you want," Rohan said.

There were sounds of laughter,
chairs pushed back, and voices
in the distance, going away.

The Willies

I asked Johan why he left home
and came to America.

How sad it can be in winter
listening to the wind . . .
No wonder that in the dawn
in the mist, one by one
figures appear among the trees,
making their way to the sea.

This is the day when the pack-boat leaves.
Better a voyage with storm and ice
than to sit in a creaking house
with a dog and old man for company.
Better a strange, hostile land,
people who do not speak your tongue,
than to listen in winter to the wind,
and look at snow on the trees.

At night when you go outside
to chop wood, you see the Willies,
those dead girls, giggling
and running. It's no dance
they mean when they crook a finger.

"You have never been to Hudik," he said.
"If you had, you'd understand.
If you heard the wind against the house,
and the voices: 'Come out, we are so lonely!'"

It's no life they have in mind for you
in a house with wife and child,
but wedding with the wind and snow.

2
LIFE ITSELF

Are you done with reviews and criticisms of life?
Animating now to life itself?

WHITMAN

Inspiration

Ars longa, vita brevis

Thank you, Jon! Your card
was just what I needed:
"The Poet's Inspiration."

He sits with his back to a tree,
in a red robe, with a wreath
of laurel on his head.

In the sky a naked cherub
is hovering, and holds out
another wreath, like a carrot . . .

the Pulitzer, I suppose.
The poet's right arm,
lifted commandingly,

points down to the tablet
a woman is pressing
against her stomach. Taking dictation . . .

I think she must be his wife . . .
eyes turned up to the sky
in wonder, her pen raised

to transcribe his every word.
On the other side of the poet
another woman stands

leaning against a tree
in a nonchalant attitude.
She is splendidly dressed,

and composed as she looks on.
A lady of leisure
apparently, the poet's muse.

A little boy stands at her side,
holding a wreath
like a plaything, to be thrown.

                    *

Poussin's "Inspiration"
has set my brain cells going.
What shall I write? For whom?

And why do we bother?
A "public for poetry" never was,
and never will be.

"Popular taste," said Whitman,
"will be taking precedence
in the arts." The old man seems

to have thought that people
would be avidly reading
the poetry of Walt Whitman.

I'm sorry, Walt, but the public
these days doesn't read anything.
The public watches TV.

                    *

That's all right by me.
Popularity out of the way,
we can get on with art. It's long.

A Wandering Life

Breathes there the man with soul so dead
Who never to himself hath said,
This is my own, my native land!

Yes, Walter, there breathes.
I recall the curse you uttered
on expatriates. The "wretch,"

though he may have power
and "pelf," whatever that means,
is "concentred all in self."

Who has not seen you on Princes Street
in kilt and sporran, the regalia
of a patriot and family man . . .

genius of the tweed shops,
the shops selling cairngorms
and a knife to put in your sock?

But what is our nation?
The place where we were born
or the one that permits us to live?

The Blue Coast

1

Peter sat in the garden
with Priscilla, Richard's wife.

"Are you always so serious?"
she said. "Talk about me.

How old would you say I am?"
"Twenty."

        She laughed
and patted him on the knee.

2

A friend of Richard's came by
and they all went to Fréjus
for dinner. Richard drove,
Jack beside him, Priscilla
with Peter in the back.

Jack and Richard reminisced.
The other ranks were splendid,
but the Colonel, what an ass.
In the back seat breathlessly
Peter and Priscilla kissed.

3

Richard said to Priscilla,
"Malcolm is driving down."
"Malcolm?" Peter said. "Who's he?"
"An old friend," said Priscilla.

Malcolm arrived. He told them
how bad things in England were.
Something under the Bentley
wanted adjusting. His legs stuck out,

Priscilla squatted in shorts,
handing him the pliers or wrench.

4

Malcolm and Priscilla
drove over to Cannes
and didn't get back
until four in the morning.

The next day Malcolm left,
disappearing in a cloud of dust.
Peter had to leave too, tomorrow.
"Why so sudden?"

"He's angry at me," said Priscilla.
"Oh is he?" Richard said.

5

He looked back from the train
at the Lavandou: rows of vines,
naked as mandrakes in April.

He unwrapped the book Richard
had given him for his journey:
Sentimental Education.

Lilies of the Field

"The road is full of people,
cars and carts, bicycles.
A Heinkel flies over . . . everyone
is screaming and running.
We too. We come to a river
with trees. We take off our shoes
and put our feet in the water.

                        "Seltsam,
alles, was sich bezog, so lose im Raum
flattern zu zehen."

                        Strange,
all that was together, now loose,
flying away in space.

        *

"You could get out of France
if you got to Marseilles.
Prix fixe. See the Chief of Police.

He was making us wait.
I said, 'May Madame sit down?'
and he doubled the price on the spot."

        *

Anna came in with a tray,
put it down, wiped her hands
on her apron, and poured tea.

She was silent while he talked,
looking at her husband
as though he were God's gift:
the long nose, lines of hair
combed across his baldness.

"My English," she said, "is no good."
Later she became less shy,
and talked about her schooldays
in Dusseldorf. She recited a poem
by Schiller, ran about in a field
with a hockey stick and shouted.

In Berlin she went to a cabaret
for the first time in her life,
and Walter was on the stage.
"He was so fine," she said. "And so handsome."

*

They are living now in Vermont.
Anna still wears her hair braided
like a schoolgirl. And Walter
leans on the gate, taking the air.

His *River of Remembrance*
sold thirteen hundred copies.
So how do they live?
Like the lilies of the field.

Travelers stop to ask directions.
"I could hardly understand a thing he said,"
they say as they drive away.
If it's Anna they talk to, on the other hand,

they have no trouble. She fitted right in,
and her English much has improved.

All Sorts of Things

All sorts of things are done in the provinces through boredom.
CHEKHOV, "THE MAN IN A CASE"

He would stoop, pick up something,
look at it, and then
let it fall. The next afternoon
there he was again, walking slowly,
or stopping to examine

whatever it was he'd found.
I asked him, "What is it?"
He held out his hand. A stone.
He said, "It's almost perfect.
Look at it." And I did.

It was green, oval-shaped.
He showed me another . . .
reddish brown. There were many
like these. On other beaches
you could hardly find them at all.

*

I talked to Connie Fisher
who's in real estate and knows.
"That's Bill Mackay,"
she said. "He and his wife
moved here from New York.

He used to be in advertising
but now he's retired.
What he needs is a regular hobby,"
she said, "like golf or a boat.
The garden keeps me on my toes."

The Floor Lamp

He threw his belongings
in one of the matching suitcases.
And the floor lamp was his.

He took a taxi to the station.
The lamp was awkward to carry.
The shade tilted like a hat.

Suppose he just left it. . . .
He could see it on the platform,
waiting for him to come back.

The early commuters
would step around it.
Later when everyone was hurrying

it would fall with a crack.
He picked up the floor lamp,
and the suitcase, and turned back.

"He's asleep"

The phone was ringing.
He looked at his watch.
2:07 A.M.

A voice said, "He's asleep."
A woman's voice. It spoke again:
"I'll be there in a minute."

Then, "Marty?"
He said, "This isn't Marty."
Then a hum. She had hung up.

His wife was awake. "Who was it?"
He said, "A wrong number,"
and she went back to sleep.

In the morning he pondered
the guests who were at breakfast
at the tables and in the booths.

Two were absorbed in the *Times*.
They had nothing to say to each other
apparently. Nothing at all.

Another couple, obviously married . . .
One would say something
and the other would nod.

This had been going on for years . . .
every thought they expressed
familiar and understood.

Or was it the one with style
having breakfast all by herself,
"he" being still asleep?

There was no way of knowing.
It could have been any of the women
in the room, except his wife.

In Country Houses

The man who was renting
the house next door, but living
apart from his wife, came back.

We heard what sounded like
a firecracker, and her voice saying,
"Put down that shotgun!"

Another shot. She shrieked.
The shriek became a continuing
high-pitched, keening sound.

Now he lies in the hospital
on a life-support system,
"brain dead" we've been told.

There is no way to find out
why the man tried to kill himself
from what we read in the paper.

Or the laughing weatherman
and the talk show at four:
"Husbands who have left their wives."

*

Everything is quiet now.
I recall something that a friend
once said: he spoke of "people

who live in country houses
at the end of drives."
I've often thought about them,

imagining what goes on
in some of those houses
in the silence of their lives.

Country Doctor

In New York, London, or Paris,
doctors have splendid offices.
It is different where we live.
You approach, through a waiting room
that is small, the doctor's office
that is even smaller still.
He is dying, to put it in a nutshell.

Head bowed over his desk
he listens to your pain,
liver or back. Wrapping the tourniquet
around your arm, he trembles
with the effort. Head bent
to your heart . . . His hand shakes
as he writes the prescription.

Some words from the Greek perhaps.

The Fence

It only took a moment
to see what a life with her
would be like. As clearly
as the corner of a roof
against the bright blue sky.

This went on for years,
with times when he or she
would be seeing someone else.

Once when she drove him to the airport
there was a wire mesh fence
separating those who had tickets
from the ones who were seeing them off.
When he looked back
she had her face pressed into the fence
and her fingers hooked around the wire.

"I don't know why I'm telling you this,"
he said. "Maybe you can use it
for one of your stories.
It's of no use to me."

At Journey's End

"And I shall dine at journey's end
With Landor and with Donne.
Can you imagine? Landor!"

He finished his martini
and looked around. The maitre d'
came over. "Monsieur?"

"This wasn't a real martini,
it was nearly all water."
The maitre d' was desolated.
He told the wine steward to bring
a real martini.

"If I had to dine at journey's end,
I'd want it to be with women,
like Paul Léautaud."

                    "Who's he?"

"Was. A writer, who worked
in a publishing house, like you."

"What did he write?"

"A novel or two. A journal.
Any time he had a few francs
he'd spend it on his animals.
He had a piece of property
that he inherited somehow,
and he kept a whole menagerie,
strays he picked up in the street,
dogs and cats, even a monkey.

He was poor and obscure all his life,
except at the end, on the radio,
when it no longer mattered.
Yet he always had some woman,
they couldn't get enough of him.
Even when he was an old man
there was one young woman
passionately in love with him."

The martini came. "Here's to us,"
he said. "May we live so long."

This martini wasn't right either.
It was nearly all vermouth,
he said, and ordered another.

Foursome

Adele said, "I know a game.
Each of us has to describe
his or her most embarrassing moment.
Then we'll all four take a vote,
and the winner will have a prize."

Joe told of going for a swim
and walking out of the showers
to find himself standing naked
at poolside, in plain view.
He had walked through the wrong door.

Maura's most embarrassing moment,
she said, was the evening
Joe's parents came to dinner.
She made a shrimp remoulade,
and ruined it entirely.

Adele's most embarrassing moment,
she said, was at Carnegie Hall,
in the *Divertimento for Strings*.
She played a wrong note, a clinker.
She could have died.

Maura was staring at Adele.
Then she said it was late
and they had to be going.
Maura and Joe are no longer
a foursome with Frank and Adele.

Wash, Dry, and Fold

Where was the top of his pajamas?
He drove back to the laundry.

She said they had washed it.
He should look for it again.
He stared at her in anger.

How would she like to go back to China
in disgrace, to her father's house?
She could hang herself from a willow.
Mournful songs would be made about her.

                    *

He found the top of his pajamas.
They had put it on a hanger
along with his shirts.

                    In China
everyone dresses in pajamas,
whether they're going fishing
or discussing Confucian philosophy.

The next time he went to the laundry
he explained to her: "In China
maybe shirt. Not in U. S. A."
He cradled his head in his hand . . .
"For sleepy time. Go along pajama."

She shook her head and turned away.
"Ah so!" he thought he heard her say.

Any Time Now

He rang the bell. Footsteps
approached. There was a pause
as an eye looked through the peephole.
Bolts were being drawn, chains were rattling.

"Come in! What are you waiting for?"
Sam said. "An invitation?"

       *

Lorraine, Sam Edelson's wife,
had big eyes. He remembered
how pretty they used to be.

"Do you remember my reviews?"
Sam said.

      "Of course. They were terrific."

"It was the best damned novel
in the fifties, with one other,
Yates's, and they buried that too.

Why am I eating hamburger helper?
And why is it, Henry Beaumont,
every time he writes a novel,
it gets on the bestseller list?"

He paused. "J. J. used to ask you
to his place in Old Greenwich."

"Yes."

"He used to ask Beaumont.
The son of a bitch never asked me."

*

"But it's OK," he said,
"things are going to change.
I finally quit fooling around
and wrote the big one, like Mario.
He plays poker with our bunch,
every Friday. He airmailed
a copy to a man he knows
on the Coast. He's reading it now.

He's a friend of Paul Newman.
You get a name to take an interest,
and the rest naturally follows.
I'm expecting a call any time.
Ask Lorraine, I can't go out.
I haven't been out of the apartment,
I have to be near the phone."

He looked at his wife. Her lips
were moving.

"Go on. Ask her!"

"Yes," she said, "a man is reading it.
He could call at any time."

Sanctuary Road

1
A Nonconforming Lot

So you bought the old place.
You ought to have talked to us.

It's on a nonconforming lot.
Anything you want to do,

you want to put in a window,
you have to ask permission,

and the village likes to say no.

2
The Roofer's Story

They were on the Verrazano
when "the truck took a wrong turn."

They found themselves on the Island,
so they just kept going.

The monkey? Some people are put off,
but there's nothing like a monkey

on the roof. It's good for business.

3
Sanctuary Road

There's nothing much to see,
and not much to discuss:

the mice running in the wall.
But every afternoon at three
they stand beside the road
waiting for the school bus,

the children, the point of it all.

Kaimana Beach

The moon with a ring
colored like a rainbow
above the ocean (Makai).

To the north (Mauka)
a mass of rosy clouds . . .
two slopes of a mountain
sprinkled with golden lights.
Looking to the west (Ewa),
high rises, here and there
showing a light. The sky
growing lighter. Beams
of a car coming down the road.
The first jogger entering the park.

So every day would begin.
They would go for a drive
inland, across the mountains,
or east around the shore,
and look at the Chinese Hat.

Or go hiking. But in a fortnight
one coconut looks much like another,
and now they pass the mornings
sitting or lying on the sand
at the Outrigger Canoe Club,
listening to the waves,
and the names of children
being called . . . "Joy!" and "Milo!"

She is beginning to miss
her office, the telephone calls;
the clean green blotting paper,
sleek black pencil holder,

rolodex, calendar,
chrome and black vinyl chair,
classically simple bud vase
from Sweden, and the traffic moving
like bugs so far below.

Lord, let us have something
to read. For there is no one
to talk to: only the sand
and a clatter of dishes,
the flapping of umbrellas,
and shadows of the afternoon.

3
THE OWNER OF THE HOUSE

Peter's Dream

There were spiders on the ladder
where he had to place his hands.

In a room with no windows
men in dustcoats were working,

carpenters with saws and hammers,
so he backed out again.

A man watching from an alcove
spoke words that were encouraging.

*

He was standing on a terrace,
looking down at the ground.

There people were walking
with slow steps, in a circle.

A woman held out her arms
as she walked, to the air

as though to embrace it.
She laughed and tossed her hair.

*

He came to his father's house.
It was silent and dark.

The sea came up to it.
The time had come for him

to set out on his journey.
The mountain saw him off,

and a tree with one arm
waved from the barren rocks.

A Walk with Goethe

One of the plainclothes policemen
handed back my wallet . . .

they were only doing their duty.
He touched his hat with two fingers.

I was going up to my room
when a light went on in my head.

All the dollars were gone,
and also my French francs.

                    *

I had a letter from the President
of the Academy of Romania.

"We hope you come back soon.
If it's any consolation,

Goethe said that every poem
had cost him a purse of gold."

A Walk with Bashō

Old boards by the sea
when the tide runs around them
still yearn to sail free.

The moon bright and round
troubles my heart. The old pond
frog-jumping-in sound.

Confessions of a Professor of English

It was beautiful in Berkeley
looking across the bay
at the lights of San Francisco.

A man from one of the oldest families,
who had lived in the Bay Area
all his life, told me, "I moved once,
to Oakland. But I moved back.
San Francisco is where it's at."
He was writing a book, *Queen City
of the Pacific.* "How do you like it?
I mean as a title?" I said
I liked it. I really did. It had a ring.

One day, during my office hour
I was reading *The Faerie Queene,*
which I detested but was required
to teach, when a pair of heels
came running down the corridor.
A young woman in a miniskirt
went sobbing by my door,
and she shouted, "Oh my God!"
People came out of their offices.
Whittaker who was in the 18th century
put out his head. "What was that?"
"I don't know," I said. "Search me."

One day Jim Anderson was shot
by a deranged former student
who walked in with a shotgun.
Jim lived, but the graduate student
who was with him, jumped up
and got the other barrel in his back,
and died on the spot.

I mention these things only because
they were so unusual. Otherwise
time just seemed to go by.

But then there was the Free Speech Movement.
While trying to teach *The Faerie Queene*
you heard the loudspeakers in the Plaza . . .
Goldberg, Aptheker, Mario Savio.
The students sat in Sproul Hall.
Joan Baez arrived, and led the way,
singing, "We Shall Overcome."
The students lay down and were carried
by policemen, and put in paddy wagons.

I left in '67, and so missed
the People's Park, helicopters spraying
students and faculty alike with tear gas.
All of that.

What a strange thing it was
to be a professor of English!
Once at a faculty meeting I heard
a professor who shall be nameless
say that D. H. Lawrence was
"an uneducated man."
Not that I like D. H. Lawrence . . .
Like the author of *The Faerie Queene*
he's one of the bastards I'm glad
I shall never have to meet.
Once he threw a little dog he had,
I think its name was Biddles,
against a rock.
But "uneducated"? Oh my god!

I do remember the faces
of some students. The happy few.
In a few years, I told them,

there'll be no more Departments
of English. Not to worry,
it will be like the Middle Ages:
enclaves of those who can read.
And when there's a famine or plague
the people will take them out and kill them.
But poetry won't die,
for there'll always be a poet.

They were listening intently,
except for the two in the back.
A colleague told me once,
"I heard some students talking about you.
One said, 'I like to hear him rave.'"

A Farewell to His Muse

The floorboards creak
and I lie thinking.
Timor mortis non conturbat me.
The idea of dying
doesn't frighten me a bit,
nor the bad road to it,
sans eyes, sans teeth. . . .

But the muse has left my bed,
having removed her things
on the sly, thinking
I don't notice, the bitch!
Go on, why don't you
just say it, "I don't love you."
Leave! Get the hell out!
I don't want to know who with.

Some talentless creep
from a Creative Writing
and Poetry Business School.
Get on line—*vita brevis*—
prostrate yourself,
crawl on hands and knees,
and kiss her *ars longa.*

He's got it all worked out:
two years to a Guggenheim,
followed by the reward
of genius, a MacArthur;
in ten, with the assistance
of friends, the Pulitzer.
Finally to sit in state
in the National Academy
and Institute of Conniving . . .

*

Well, easy come,
easy go. And it's been fun.
Farewell the something something
that make ambition virtue.

There was a time I could quote
the Bard by the yard,
but I had to give it up.
There is nothing you can learn
from the English, except
how to talk like a gentleman
with your nose in the air
and marbles in your mouth.

In fact, there was nothing
I could learn from anyone.
All you really know is given
at moments when you're seeing
and listening.

       Being in love
is a great help.

Oh yes, but keep a dog.

Footnotes to Fodor's *Spain*

1

Start, everyone does, from the Prado.
The painter of the *aristos*
gaily in blue and rose
also painted the Third of May:
prisoners being herded
like cattle up the hill;
the firing squad bending
intently to take aim;
the *insurrecto* who opens
his arms wide to his death.
But this other is no hero:
he looks at it out of the corner
of an eye, and bites his fingers.

And witches, the old ones . . .
Their hideous features ask,
Why have we been damned?
Are we not also His children?

And the half-buried dog,
head and neck straining
at heaven, that light!
Can it be that in all the universe
there is no one, nothing that sees and cares?

2

Work in the morning,
in the afternoon make love.
Eat at Casa Botin,

Calle Chuchilleros 17,
the fish casserole, it's good.

3

When you sit in the plaza
you are accosted by, in this order:
a beggar of middle age
who hovers and won't leave—
when your wife says "No,"
he answers, "Why no?"

a deaf-and-dumb man
with a card that says "Poet,"
a beggar woman in black,
another poet . . . this one mutters,
a Gypsy with an infant on her back,
a Gypsy boy, and others.

4

In Seville, across from the Cathedral,
you can discover America,
forest, farm and mine
on paper, ten thousand volumes!

A clerk would copy the report
written in malaria by a shaking hand,
of savages, snakes, and crocodiles,
and how, in this place, there was gold.

Señor, the only El Dorado
I have ever seen was the filling
in the smile of a tax collector.

How neat and clear it is,
the mapping and the writing,
the lines on the paper
moving in light like the sea.

5

"The most intelligent man in Europe"
explained the decline of the economy.
He said, "Listen carefully.
The interest in the national debt
is now equal to the entire budget
under Franco: 700 million."

He spoke of the disasters of socialism,
the responsibility of the U.S.
to Europe. "It's not Texas
or Maine that's at stake when you vote
but Spain, France, Holland . . . all of liberty."
But when he spoke of "the mistake
you made in the Philippines
by not supporting Marcos,"
your attention wandered
to the crows making a racket
nearby in the public gardens.

6

Juan Ramón Jiménez

In order to get to Moguer
you will have to go to Huelva.
You can wait in the café
where flies walk on the cakes
and a boy who walks on crutches

because he has no feet, only stumps,
places a hand on the table
for balance, and asks for a cigarette.

Let us say, you arrive at Moguer . . .
There's the statue, it could be anyone's,
and his books. He would laugh and swear
and write in the margins.

There was a story he liked to tell.
A poet was passing through Avila. . . .
He pointed to a tree, "What is it?"
"That," he was told, "is the alamo.
You know, the tree you are always
writing about in your poems."

A pen, a watch, eyeglasses,
the box from which the donkey
is said to have eaten hay . . .

The walk they used to take together?
The people who own the land
have fenced it off. Forget it!

Homeless Men

I stopped for the light.
A bearded face
crossed the street,
glaring at us. "Hurstwood,"

I said. My companion,
after a pause, answered,
"I tried to read the book.
I couldn't make it to the end."

The light changed
and we drove on.
He couldn't take the story,
he said, it was too real.

He could just see himself
making a mistake like Hurstwood,
and falling, step by step
to the bottom. Lying in the gutter.

*

He's worked his way from Houston
up Broadway. There he is again,
outside a restaurant, looking in
at the gleams of glass and silver. . . .

"Go on," he says, talking
to the air, "stuff your faces.
Don't think of anybody else.
Enjoy yourselves while you can,

you don't know what you may come to."
He laughs. A passing couple

stare at him, he stares back,
and they walk past in a hurry.

*

The man I was driving with that night
who couldn't finish the book,
went on to make a complete mess
of his life.

There are no second acts
in American lives,
Fitzgerald said. He was wrong.
When the curtain went up again

Roger was there for Act Two,
with a new wife and a new career.
The world is so full of a number of things . . .
the trick is not to let it get to you.

*

Where is the Union Captain
who used to stand on a corner
soliciting for us all?
He understood the wind and snow.

"This man must have a bed,"
and someone crossed the street
and gave him twelve cents. When
he had enough money

for all of us, and not till then,
he would march his ragtag bobtail army
off to bed. Hooray for the Union!

In the Alpha Cradle

The flesh is sad, alas!
and I have read all the magazines.

My name being called . . . at last!
I lie beneath the gantry,

looking up at the head
and arm, the catcher's mitt.

The head is peering at me.
Chris or Angie slides a block,

translucent plastic, into the slot.
They go scurrying off

and hide behind the wall.
The gantry makes a beeping sound.

They come scurrying back,
Sneezy, Bashful, and Doc.

The head and arm swing around.
They slide in another block.

*

At the edge of the parking lot
two men are managing to lift

an enormously fat man out of a van . . .
wedging him into a wheelchair.

He is swearing and waving his arms.
To go to so much trouble . . .

Something or someone
must love him very much.

Reading the Times

I'm reading about this man in Ohio,
an "assembler."

He says, "I have five kids,
three grandkids . . . a Mustang,

a Firebird, a Ford Ranger,
an '89 Camaro, a '92 Chevy van

at 8.9 percent interest,
a color T.V., a V.C.R.

and a Nintendo.
Am I doing good or what?"

                    *

It was just like a movie,
they said yesterday in L. A.

Two men in black with body armor
shot it out with the police.

Two thumbs up. A four-star thriller!
There's so much going on.

It's like *The Wizard of Oz:*
a house flies by, then a witch.

Then it settles, and everything
is right back where it was.

The *Wow!* Factor

"It's the *Wow!* factor."
And how about this for the name

of a program, *The Speed of Time?*
I said, "But what does it mean?"

They voted for it anyway.
And what Charley Baker said

in the conference room
that day, to the C.E.O. . . . .

"I don't know what you're thinking
but I'm thinking the same thing."

     *

I've taken to fly-fishing.
Wading out in the river

up to your waist. Casting
so that it doesn't splash

and spook every fish in a mile.
It's quiet. The only sound,

water rushing over a stone;
the dead branch of a tree

in the forest tearing and falling
somewhere, a long way off.

Driving

The long line of cars and trucks
in front appears to be moving

up to an edge. They go over
one by one, and disappear,

falling into the dark valley
of dry bones and scrap metal.

Yet some poor fool behind you
in the line keeps blowing his horn.

A Shearling Coat

Alexander Ortiz and Arlyne Gonzales
were walking home from a movie.

A car drew up, and two men
got out. One had a gun, the other

tugged at her shearling coat.
"Don't hurt her," Ortiz said, "she's pregnant."

The gunman shot him twice,
in the chest and throat.

"What you do that for?" said the other.
"C'mon, c'mon, get the jacket,"

the gunman said, and they left,
with a parting shot at Gonzales.

She had thrown herself down
on top of the dying man.

And I shall be wanting to be rid
of this thing to the end of my days.

Graduation

My ex-wife comes over
and invites me to sit

with them. I say okay.
There are a lot of speeches,

all saying much the same,
about the new generation,

the future belongs to them.
They're lining up for it,

walking onto the stage.
There she is, our Meredith.

The sound of two hands clapping
is mine. If there's one thing I know

it's when something is over and
done with, and it's time to go.

Variations on a Theme by Shostakovich

Galich . . . the name leapt at me
from a shelf. It's a sign,
I said to myself.
But his real name was Ginzburg.

It's not such a good idea
to be a Jew in Russia.
He took the name of a teacher
of the great poet Pushkin.

For he too was a poet,
though mainly he wrote plays,
about mixups, misunderstandings,
romance . . . that kind of thing.

They were enormously successful.
Moreover, he was handsome
and charming. "The most popular man
in Russia," somebody said.

*

These were the years when Stalin
was shunting people off
to Siberia, where they died.

The time of Virta's "no conflict theory" . . .
There could be no conflict in plays
written in the Soviet Union:
there was only a struggle
between the "good" and the "better."

Galich titled one of his plays
Moscow Does Not Believe in Tears.

But let him tell it himself:
"Many times, many ways, we played silent parts,
and our silence meant 'yes' and not 'no'."

*

Josef Stain died at last,
but his pall-bearers clung
to power, like lice in a coat.

Galich sang openly
of the lies and injustices
he saw in the life around him.

He joined the Orthodox Church.
A "Committee for Human Rights"!
Sasha, where are you going?

He signed an open letter
calling for amnesty
for all political prisoners.

He called for repeal of the law
that prohibited Jews from emigrating.
Ginzburg, you'd better look out!

*

To the meeting of the Writers' Union
to discuss Galich's behavior
came a man named Arbuzov.

He had it in for Galich.
The members of a collective
had written a play . . . Arbuzov
published it under his name.
Galich spoke of this with contempt.

The meeting of the tribunal
gave Arbuzov his chance.
He shed tears . . . he was shaken,
he said, at having to bear witness
to the depths to which the man had sunk.

The meeting became a celebration
of Arbuzov, and Galich was expelled,
cast out of the Writers' Union.
He would not be permitted
to publish his work from now on.

And then he was banned
by the Litfond, the body
that gave financial aid to writers.

                    *

At the corner of Sadovaya Street
Galich ran into three men
who were out for a good time.
They knocked off his hat.

"You old *git*," they said,
"when are you going to leave the country?"
"What do you mean?"
he stammered. "This is my home."

But he and his wife were starving.
After several applications
they had a permit to leave . . .
at once, within twenty-four hours.

They did, and were made welcome
in Norway. Then they traveled
through Europe, Galich performing
his songs to the guitar.

Finally they made their home in Paris.

*

He was doing something with a wire
and the tape recorder.

He put the plug in a socket
and saw the domes of Moscow

shining like peeled onions,
pfft! and he was dead.

"Isn't that your hat?"
Pushkin said. He picked it up,

brushed it with his sleeve,
and put it on Galich's head.

At the Church Door

I didn't stay for the closing
hymns and prayers. I felt
out of sorts, so I left.

Someone was before me
at the door: a child, gazing
at a spot on her wrist.

She said, "Can you help me?"
"What is it?"
"A ladybug," she said.

So I opened the door,
and she said, "It jumped off."
We stood looking around.

"It'll be all right," I said.
She went in, and I left,
taking care where I stepped.

The Children's Choir

The voices of the children
singing in the cupola
still sing every Sunday.

A woman conducts them
with fingers pointing up.
She tugs at her earlobe.

I wouldn't be surprised
if the choir were to rise
and fly through a window.

It's too beautiful for words.
But one of the children
yawns a round O.

And so we are spared
the opening of the sky
and the end of the world.

Grand Forks

The old woman who still
bears some strong vestiges
of former beauty, once
played Broadway in *Hello, Dolly!*
and toured with a road company.

Now she lives alone. For company
she has three dogs, an unspecified
number of cats, and animals
passing through with broken limbs,
wounds, or contusions.

As there is no veterinarian
for miles, she injects them
with the necessary medication,
and binds up their wounds.

                    *

Here genocide once planted its flag,
but has been rooted out. Murder
and rape still make an appearance,
but these are isolated cases.

What is usual is silence,
or a creaking board.
The wind blows across the land
with no letup. A fence
cuts the wind, and the wind closes around it.

The old woman who lives
out here all alone,
who has seen and known so much,

is taking a course in writing.
She told me so herself.

In this place it is clear that the word
is with us, and nowhere else.

The Owner of the House

The movers came, and took
her bed, table, everything,
until the house was empty.

She was walking on a road
at night, in a dark dress,
and so she was hit.

A driver who had seen it
said that he thought someone
threw a doll up in the air.

*

I found some smaller things
that had been overlooked.
A fish made of wood.

A bell, perhaps for calling
a cat. Every night
one comes around and mourns.

A hidden drawer with thread
and needle, thimble, things
as hidden as a heart.

*

She let the house run down,
the garden be overgrown,
lost in her arcane studies.

They had to do with the eye
of a fish that she had found
somewhere in Mexico.

A neighbor disconnected
the refrigerator, but did not
think to empty it. Fishes stink.

*

I open the door of a cabinet
and forget to close it again—
whack! The side of my head.

"Just to remind you,"
she whispers, "it's my house."
The carpenters are hard at work—

I need more space. She stands
watching a while, and leaves.
She'll have the run of it still.

from
THE ARRIVISTES: POEMS 1940–1949

1949
✳

Arm in Arm

Arm in arm in the Dutch dyke
Were piled both friend and foe
With rifle, helmet, motor-bike:
Step over as you go.

They laid the Captain on a bed
Of gravel and green grass.
The little Dutch girl held his head
And motioned us to pass.

Her busy hands seemed smooth as silk
To a soldier in the sun,
When she gave him a jug of milk
In which his blood did run.

O, had the Captain been around
When trenching was begun,
His bright binoculars had found
The enemy's masked gun!

Beside a Church we dug our holes,
By tombstone and by cross.
They were too shallow for our souls
When the ground began to toss.

Which were the new, which the old dead
It was a sight to ask.
One private found a polished head
And took the skull to task

For spying on us. Till along
Driving the clouds like sheep,
Our bombers came in a great throng:
And so we fell asleep.

Lazarus Convalescent

These are the evening hours and he walks
Down to the Hudson, to that lonesome river,
And while a piano plays he sits and talks.
"Do you remember Judson?
Huge cloudy symbols of a high romance . . .
I think he went into insurance."

The water laps, the seagulls plunge and squawk
And lovers lock in wind that makes him shiver.
"I'll have to learn to use a knife and fork
Again. Look there above us!
Spry's for Baking . . . starry spectacle.
For Frying. More, a miracle."

Perhaps at running water he can balk
The bloodhound that is howling for his liver.
Now he will rise again, rise up and walk.
"And do you know, I've found
My neighbors spy on me when I undress.
Perhaps I ought to change, to change my address."

He sees his oracle, the weight machine.
His flesh is right; he laughs and pats the giver.
Alas, its entrails also tell his fortune,
Turning him ghastly white.
He moves from all his friends with a cursed stealth.
What has the mouth informed him? "Guard your health."

Summer Storm

In that so sudden summer storm they tried
Each bed, couch, closet, carpet, car-seat, table,
Both river banks, five fields, a mountain side,
Covering as much ground as they were able.

A lady, coming on them in the dark
In a white fixture, wrote to the newspapers
Complaining of the statues in the park.
By Cupid, but they cut some pretty capers!

The envious oxen in still rings would stand
Ruminating. Their sweet incessant plows
I think had changed the contours of the land
And made two modest conies move their house.

God rest them well, and firmly shut the door.
Now they are married Nature breathes once more.

A Witty War

Oh, we loved long and happily, God knows!
A witty war that flourished seven years,
Where the small river to the ocean flows.
Our quarrel made us kiss, kisses brought cares,
And closeness caused the taking off of clothes.
Oh, we loved long and happily, God knows!

"The watchdogs are asleep, the doormen doze!"
We made our own sweet music on the stairs.
Lightly we stepped and little stood to lose;
We had our own, and the world its, affairs . . .
Or so we said while taking off our clothes.
Oh, we loved long and happily, God knows!

Between us two a silent treason grows.
Our eyes are empty, or they meet with tears.
Wild is the wind, from a cold country blows,
In which our tender greenness disappears.
And did this come of taking off our clothes?
Oh, we loved long and happily, God knows!

The bells beginning gladly, at the close
Tongue sullenly. Your jetty shining hair
And your brown eyes would be the worst of foes,
For they know when to strike my heart and where.
This nakedness is all our own, God knows,
And shall remain till time makes us some clothes.

Carentan O Carentan

Trees in the old days used to stand
And shape a shady lane
Where lovers wandered hand in hand
Who came from Carentan.

This was the shining green canal
Where we came two by two
Walking at combat-interval.
Such trees we never knew.

The day was early June, the ground
Was soft and bright with dew.
Far away the guns did sound,
But here the sky was blue.

The sky was blue, but there a smoke
Hung still above the sea
Where the ships together spoke
To towns we could not see.

Could you have seen us through a glass
You would have said a walk
Of farmers out to turn the grass,
Each with his own hay-fork.

The watchers in their leopard suits
Waited till it was time,
And aimed between the belt and boot
And let the barrel climb.

I must lie down at once, there is
A hammer at my knee.
And call it death or cowardice,
Don't count again on me.

Everything's all right, Mother,
Everyone gets the same
At one time or another.
It's all in the game.

I never strolled, nor ever shall,
Down such a leafy lane.
I never drank in a canal,
Nor ever shall again.

There is a whistling in the leaves
And it is not the wind,
The twigs are falling from the knives
That cut men to the ground.

Tell me, Master-Sergeant,
The way to turn and shoot.
But the Sergeant's silent
That taught me how to do it.

O Captain, show us quickly
Our place upon the map.
But the Captain's sickly
And taking a long nap.

Lieutenant, what's my duty,
My place in the platoon?
He too's a sleeping beauty,
Charmed by that strange tune.

Carentan O Carentan
Before we met with you
We never yet had lost a man
Or known what death could do.

Song: "Rough Winds Do Shake the Darling Buds of May"

Rough winds do shake
                do shake
                          the darling buds of May
The darling buds
                rose-buds
                      the winds do shake
That are her breasts,
Those darling buds, dew-tipped, her sighing moods do shake.

She is sixteen
                sixteen
                      and her young lust
Is like a thorn
                hard thorn
                      among the pink
Of her soft nest.
Upon this thorn she turns, for love's incessant sake.

Her heart will break
                  will break
                      unless she may
Let flow her blood
                red blood
                      to ease the ache
Where she is pressed.
Then she'll lie still, asleep, who now lies ill, awake.

Well I have seen
                have seen
                      one come to joust
Who has a horn
                sweet horn,

                    and spear to sink
Before he rests.
When such young buds are torn, the best true loves they make.

from
GOOD NEWS OF DEATH AND OTHER POEMS

1955

As Birds Are Fitted to the Boughs

As birds are fitted to the boughs
That blossom on the tree
And whisper when the south wind blows—
So was my love to me.

And still she blossoms in my mind
And whispers softly, though
The clouds are fitted to the wind,
The wind is to the snow.

A Woman Too Well Remembered

Having put on new fashions, she demands
New friends. She trades her beauty and her humor
In anybody's eyes. If diamonds
Were dark, they'd sparkle so. Her aura is
The glance of scandal and the speed of rumor.

One day, as I recall, when we conversed
In kisses, it amused her to transmit
"What hath God wrought!"—the message that was first
Sent under the Atlantic. Nonsense, yet
It pleases me sometimes to think of it.

Noli me tangere was not her sign.
Her pilgrim trembled with the softest awe.
She was the only daughter of a line
That sleeps in poetry and silences.
She might have sat upon the Sphinx's paw.

Then is she simply false, and falsely fair?
(The promise she would break she never made)
I cannot say, but truly can compare,
For when the stars move like a steady fire
I think of her, and other faces fade.

The Man Who Married Magdalene

The man who married Magdalene
Had not forgiven her
God might pardon every sin . . .
Love is no pardoner.

Her hands were hollow, pale, and blue,
Her mouth like watered wine.
He watched to see if she were true
And waited for a sign.

It was old harlotry, he guessed,
That drained her strength away,
So gladly for the dark she dressed,
So sadly for the day.

Their quarrels made her dull and weak
And soon a man might fit
A penny in the hollow cheek
And never notice it.

At last, as they exhausted slept,
Death granted the divorce,
And nakedly the woman leapt
Upon that narrow horse.

But when he woke and woke alone
He wept and would deny
The loose behavior of the bone
And the immodest thigh.

Memories of a Lost War

The guns know what is what, but underneath
In fearful file
We go around burst boots and packs and teeth
That seem to smile.

The scene jags like a strip of celluloid,
A mortar fires,
Cinzano falls, Michelin is destroyed,
The man of tires.

As darkness drifts like fog in from the sea
Somebody says
"We're digging in." Look well, for this may be
The last of days.

Hot lightnings stitch the blind eye of the moon,
The thunder's blunt.
We sleep. Our dreams pass in a faint platoon
Toward the front.

Sleep well, for you are young. Each tree and bush
Drips with sweet dew,
And earlier than morning June's cool hush
Will waken you.

The riflemen will wake and hold their breath.
Though they may bleed
They will be proud a while of something death
Still seems to need.

The Heroes

I dreamed of war-heroes, of wounded war-heroes
With just enough of their charms shot away
To make them more handsome. The women moved nearer
To touch their brave wounds and their hair streaked with gray.

I saw them in long ranks ascending the gangplanks;
The girls with the doughnuts were cheerful and gay.
They minded their manners and muttered their thanks;
The Chaplain advised them to watch and to pray.

They shipped these rapscallions, these seasick battalions
To a patriotic and picturesque spot;
They gave them new bibles and marksmen's medallions,
Compasses, maps, and committed the lot.

A fine dust has settled on all that scrap metal.
The heroes were packaged and sent home in parts
To pluck at a poppy and sew on a petal
And count the long night by the stroke of their hearts.

The Battle

Helmet and rifle, pack and overcoat
Marched through a forest. Somewhere up ahead
Guns thudded. Like the circle of a throat
The night on every side was turning red.

They halted and they dug. They sank like moles
Into the clammy earth between the trees.
And soon the sentries, standing in their holes,
Felt the first snow. Their feet began to freeze.

At dawn the first shell landed with a crack.
Then shells and bullets swept the icy woods.
This lasted many days. The snow was black.
The corpses stiffened in their scarlet hoods.

Most clearly of that battle I remember
The tiredness in eyes, how hands looked thin
Around a cigarette, and the bright ember
Would pulse with all the life there was within.

The Ash and the Oak

When men discovered freedom first
The fighting was on foot,
They were encouraged by their thirst
And promises of loot,
And when it feathered and bows boomed
Their virtue was a root.

O the ash and the oak and the willow tree
And green grows the grass on the infantry!

At Malplaquet and Waterloo
They were polite and proud,
They primed their guns with billets-doux
And, as they fired, bowed.
At Appomattox too, it seems
Some things were understood.

O the ash and the oak and the willow tree
And green grows the grass on the infantry!

But at Verdun and at Bastogne
There was a great recoil,
The blood was bitter to the bone
The trigger to the soul,
And death was nothing if not dull,
A hero was a fool.

O the ash and the oak and the willow tree
And that's an end of the infantry!

West

On US 101
I felt the traffic running like a beast,
Roaring in space.

Tamalpais
The red princess slopes
In honeyed burial from hair to feet;
The sharp lifting fog
Uncurtains Richmond and the ridge
—With two red rubies set upon the bridge—
And curtains them again.

Ranching in Bolinas, that's the life,
If you call cattle life.
To sit on a veranda with a glass
And see the sprinklers watering your land
And hear the peaches dropping from the trees
And hear the ocean in the redwood trees,

The whales of time,
Masts of the long voyages of earth,
In whose tall branches day
Hangs like a Christmas toy.

On their red columns drowse
The eagles battered at the Western gate;
These trees have held the eagles in their state
When Rome was still a rumor in the boughs.

Early in the Morning

Early in the morning
The dark Queen said,
"The trumpets are warning
There's trouble ahead."
Spent with carousing,
With wine-soaked wits,
Antony drowsing
Whispered, "It's
Too cold a morning
To get out of bed."

The army's retreating,
The fleet has fled,
Caesar is beating
His drums through the dead.
"Antony, horses!
We'll get away,
Gather our forces
For another day."
"It's a cold morning,"
Antony said.

Caesar Augustus
Cleared his phlegm.
"Corpses disgust us.
Cover them."
Caesar Augustus
In his time lay
Dying, and just as
Cold as they,
On the cold morning
Of a cold day.

from
A DREAM OF GOVERNORS

1959

I Dreamed That in a City Dark as Paris

I dreamed that in a city dark as Paris
I stood alone in a deserted square.
The night was trembling with a violet
Expectancy. At the far edge it moved
And rumbled; on that flickering horizon
The guns were pumping color in the sky.

There was the Front. But I was lonely here,
Left behind, abandoned by the army.
The empty city and the empty square
Was my inhabitation, my unrest.
The helmet with its vestige of a crest,
The rifle in my hands, long out of date,
The belt I wore, the trailing overcoat
And hobnail boots, were those of a *poilu.*
I was the man, as awkward as a bear.

Over the rooftops where cathedrals loomed
In speaking majesty, two aeroplanes
Forlorn as birds appeared. Then growing large,
The German *Taube* and the *Nieuport Scout,*
They chased each other tumbling through the sky,
Till one streamed down on fire to the earth.

These wars have been so great, they are forgotten
Like the Egyptian dynasts. My confrere
In whose thick boots I stood, were you amazed
To wander through my brain four decades later
As I have wandered in a dream through yours?

The violence of waking life disrupts
The order of our death. Strange dreams occur,
For dreams are licensed as they never were.

A Dream of Governors

The deepest dream is of mad governors.

MARK VAN DOREN

The Knight from the world's end
Cut off the dragon's head.
The monster's only friend,
The Witch, insulting, fled.
The Knight was crowned, and took
His Lady. Good and gay,
They lived in a picture book
Forever and a day.

Or else: When he had sat
So long, the King was old
And ludicrous and fat.
At feasts when poets told
How he had shed the blood
Of dragons long ago
He thought, Have I done good
To hear that I did so?

The chorus in a play
Declaimed: "The soul does well
Keeping the middle way."
He thought, That city fell;
Man's life is founded on
Folly at the extreme;
When all is said and done
The City is a dream.

At night the King alone
Went to the dragon's cave.
In moonlight on a stone
The Witch sat by the grave.

He grasped her by the hand
And said, "Grant what I ask.
Bring evil on the land
That I may have a task!"

The Queen has heard his tread;
She shuts the picture book.
The King stands by the bed.
In silence as they look
Into each other's eyes
They see a buried thing
That creeps, begins to rise,
And spreads the dragon's wing.

To the Western World

A siren sang, and Europe turned away
From the high castle and the shepherd's crook.
Three caravels went sailing to Cathay
On the strange ocean, and the captains shook
Their banners out across the Mexique Bay.

And in our early days we did the same.
Remembering our fathers in their wreck
We crossed the sea from Palos where they came
And saw, enormous to the little deck,
A shore in silence waiting for a name.

The treasures of Cathay were never found.
In this America, this wilderness
Where the axe echoes with a lonely sound,
The generations labor to possess
And grave by grave we civilize the ground.

Hot Night on Water Street

A hot midsummer night on Water Street—
The boys in jeans were combing their blond hair,
Watching the girls go by on tired feet;
And an old woman with a witch's stare
Cried "Praise the Lord!" She vanished on a bus
With hissing air brakes like an incubus.

Three hardware stores, a barbershop, a bar,
A movie playing Westerns—where I went
To see a dream of horses called *The Star* . . .
Some day, when this uncertain continent
Is marble, and men ask what was the good
We lived by, dust may whisper "Hollywood."

Then back along the river bank on foot
By moonlight. On the West Virginia side
An owlish train began to huff and hoot;
It seemed to know of something that had died.
I didn't linger— sometimes when I travel
I think I'm being followed by the Devil.

At the newsstand in the lobby, a cigar
Was talkative: "Since I've been in this town
I've seen one likely woman, and a car
As she was crossing Main Street, knocked her down."
I was a stranger here myself, I said,
And bought the *New York Times,* and went to bed.

The Boarder

The time is after dinner. Cigarettes
       Glow on the lawn;
Glasses begin to tinkle; TV sets
       Have been turned on.

The moon is brimming like a glass of beer
       Above the town,
And love keeps her appointments—"Harry's here!"
       "I'll be right down."

But the pale stranger in the furnished room
       Lies on his back
Looking at paper roses, how they bloom,
       And ceilings crack.

Orpheus in America

I

Here are your meadows, Love, as wide as heaven,
Green spirits, leaves
And winds, your ministers!

Item: a ship, that on the outer shoals
Lies broken. Item: thirty-seven souls,
Or rather, thirty-seven kinds of fever.
Item: three Indians, chained leg to leg.
Item: my lute.

This is the New England—rocks and brush
Where none may live but only tigers, parrots,
And mute imagining—
America, a desert with a name.

America begins antiquity.
Confronted with pure space, my Arcady
Has turned to stone.
Rome becomes Rome; Greece, Greece; the cottages
Collapse in ruin.

It darkens like a lapse of memory.
Here are no palaces, but lifted stone,
The pyramids of Egypt, steles
Of Ur. Columns that death has set
At the entrance to his kingdom.

II

This gazing freedom is the basilisk.
O for a mirror!

The melancholy of the possible
Unmeasures me.

Let music then begin. And let the air
Be passing sweet,
Music that scarcely wakes
The serpent in her trance

And leads the lion out into the dance.
And let the trees be moved
And may the forest dance.

Then shall intelligence and grace
Join hands and sing: goodbye to Arcady!
Anther world is here, a greener Thrace!
Here are your meadows, Love, as wide as heaven,
Green spirits, leaves
And winds, your ministers,
In this America, this other, happy place.

Music in Venice

Dismiss the instruments that for your pleasure
Have played allegro all through Italy.
Pay the musicians. Even let the poet
      Have part his pay.
For here is Venice—floating, and suspended
From purple clouds. Dismiss the music school!
Here anyone at all can play the fool
      In his own way.

Then thread the labyrinth of narrow streets,
Bridges, canals, windows of lace and glass,
High lattices that spill the scent of almonds.
      The Minotaur
That lurks in this maze is kind. An Aschenbach
Round every corner is pursuing Eros.
"Love!" cry the naked offspring of the heroes
      On the wet stone floor.

It's night in the Piazza. Lighted space
Burns like your brandy. Violins and brass
Play waltzes, fox-trots. On a cloud, St. Mark's
      Winged lion perches;
High palaces go sailing to the moon,
Which, as advertised, is perfectly clear.
The lovers rise, moon-struck, and whisper their
      Arrivedercis.

A prince of Venice, tangled in the eyes
Of a young courtesan, once staged a masque:
"The Banishment of Love." A boy like Eros
      Was rowed in chains,
Weeping, down the canal. The merchant's Venice
Splintered the Turk and swept him from her shores.
But Eros came, Eros with many oars,
      And Eros reigns.

Venice, the city built on speculation,
Still stands on it. Love sails from India
And Sweden—every hanging cloud pours out
      A treasure chest.
It's love on the Rialto, news of love
That gives Antonio his golden life,
Even to Envy, sharpening a knife,
      His interest.

Côte d'Azur

Christian says, "You know, it's Paradise,"
Mending his net.
"The English," he says, "for example.
They come and lie in the sun until they are
As red as that roof.
And then it's finished. They never recover."

The howling native children,
Roland, Giorgio, Josette, plunge in the sea,
Scramble on a raft, inspect
The official from Lyons with his glass rod
And nylon gear.
                    "I know," Roland informs him,
"Where you could have bought all that much cheaper.
That's not much of a rod."
                              "And you,"
Replies the head of the bureau
To his tormentor, "What kind of a rod
Do *you* have?"
                    Roland shrugs.
"Me?" he says. "I don't have all that money."

And here comes an excursion *en famille*.
First, they erect a yellow canvas tent
Which swallows them. Then mama-pig comes out
On her white trotters; whining daughter-pig;
Boy-pig and Baby. Look, the blossoming
Of beach-umbrellas, uncollapsing of chairs!
And last emerges the head of the family,
His face encased in glass, his feet
Froglike in flippers.
Out of his head a kind of man-from-Mars
Tube curls; his right hand grasps a trident
For finding the sea urchin. *Me voici!*

Here and there on the beach the solitary
Brood in the sun—Dutchman and Swede;
An actress in dark glasses
Reading a book; heroes and heroines
Of melodramas that are to be played:
The shot in the hotel; the speech
From a platform; the performance
Of Bach that brings the audience to their feet
Roaring in Dusseldorf.

Humankind, says the poet, cannot bear
Too much reality.
                    Nor pleasure.
And nothing is more melancholy
Than to watch people enjoying themselves
As much as they can.
                    The trick is to be busy
Mending your net, like Christian,
Or active as the father is out there
With all his tackle.

                    Look! he's caught
An octopus.

                    The children come running,
And even the Swede
Stands up to look; the actress
Smiles; and the official from Lyons
Forgets himself in the general excitement.

The Runner

This is the story of a soldier of the 101st Airborne Division of the Army of the United States.

The Runner *is fiction; the episodes and characters are imaginary. But the fiction is based on the following history.*

On September 7, 1944, parachute and glider infantry of the First British Airborne Division, the American 82nd and 101st Airborne Divisions, and a Polish brigade, descended in eastern Holland at Eindhoven, Grave, Nijmegen, and Arnhem. Their object was to make a bridgehead across the Lower Rhine at Arnhem. The British Second Army would join them and advance from Arnhem into the plains of northern Germany.

At Arnhem the British airborne troops were attacked by enemy units in overwhelming strength and forced back across the river. The more fortunate Americans defended a corridor from Eindhoven to Nijmegen. The fighting, bitter at first, settled into a stalemate and, with the coming of the rainy season, petered out entirely.

In mid-Novmber the 82nd and 101st were drawn back to Rheims, to re-equip and get the drizzle out of their bones.

On December 17 they were alerted for combat. A German attack was developing in Belgium. The divisions were hurried by truck into the Ardennes, and on the night of December 19 the 101st were digging in around Bastogne.

This poem is for Donald Hall who encouraged me to write it.

1

"And the condemned man ate a hearty meal,"
The runner said. He took his mess kit over
To the garbage can. He scraped his mess kit out,
Then dipped it in the can of soapy water,
And swished it in the can of clean, hot water,
And came back to his place.

The company
Was spread along one edge of the airfield,
Finishing lunch. Those with the appetite
Were going through the chow line once again.
They looked all pockets, pockets and baggy pants.
They held their mess kits out to the sweating cooks,
Who filled them up, then bore their precious load
Apart.

The runner felt in his breast pocket
For cigarettes. He lit one and inhaled.
Leaning back on his pack, his feet sprawled out,
He stared at the ranks of gliders and towplanes
And said, "I wonder if . . ."

"Agh!" said a voice,

"Why don't you dry up, Dodd!"

He looked around
And met the eyes of Kass, the radioman,
Glaring beneath the rim of his steel helmet.

"What?" said the runner.

"Who needs your remarks?
First, the condemned men eat a hearty meal,
And then you wonder . . ."

"When we're coming back."
"What's it to you?"

The runner didn't answer.
Sometimes it seemed that anything he said
Rubbed someone the wrong way. He'd only meant
He hoped the outfit would come back to England
And London, where he'd gone on two-day passes.

He liked the pubs, the mugs of mild-and-bitter,
And country lanes. Some day, when they came back
He'd go off on his own. Rent a bicycle.
He'd see some of the country by himself.
And if he got to London . . .

                      With a roar
An engine started. Other engines followed.
A gale from the propellers swept around him.

"Fall in!" said the First Sergeant.

                      Dodd got up
And hoisted on his pack.

                "Get a move on!"

That's how it was: you always had to wait,
And then you had to hurry. He closed his belt,
And slung his rifle over his right shoulder.
The section formed.

              "Where's Wheeler?" said the sergeant.
And here came Wheeler at a run. "You, Wheeler . . ."
The sergeant followed him with imprecations
As Wheeler ducked in place at Dodd's right hand.
Out of the side of his mouth: "Look what I got,"
Said Wheeler, and he showed in his clenched fist
A bundle of the new invasion money.
"Over in F Company," he whispered.
"The dice was really hot."

              "Ten-*hut!* For-*ard*
Arch!" said the sergeant, and they started off
Across the concrete runway. It seemed long.
Dodd's mouth was dry; his legs were weak. At last
They came up to the glider, their box kite—

High wings and rudder, little wheels that hardly
Lifted it off the ground—a canvas coffin.
Ungainly as a duck, it wouldn't fly
Unless it had to.

          Through the open door
Under the wing they climbed up one by one,
Toppling with their burdens. Found their seats.
And sat in two rows, looking at each other.
Dodd fastened his safety belt and clasped his gun
Between his knees. The Captain entered last.
They waited. The glider trembled in the blast
Of wind from the towplane. The pilots entered,
Leaping up lightly, and made their way forward
To the controls.

           The runner could see nothing
Beyond the glider's high, transparent nose;
But now, he thought, the towplane would be turning
Into the wind. Two men would run the cable
Back from the plane and hook it to the glider.
Then, with a louder blast of the propellers,
The plane would start to roll.

             The glider jerked
Forward, and rolled, creaking, and gathered speed.
The bumping stopped, and with a sudden lightness
They were airborne. Constricted where he sat,
Dodd prayed to nothing in particular:
Let the rope hold; no current whirl us down
Smashing on concrete.

           They were well away.
He stared at the slender pilots in their pinks
And sporty caps and glasses; at their hands
On the half-wheel. His life was in those hands.
He thought of shell bursts, the green canvas torn,

Men writhing in their belts, the pilots' hands
Fallen from the controls, a sickening drop.
And then he thought of fields with pointed stakes
That would shear through the sides. Of plunging out
Into machine-gun fire.

2

          "We're almost there,"
The next man said.

          The pilots were peering down.
One nodded, and the other raised his hand
And grasped the lever that released the cable,
And pulled it down.

          The glider soared, then fell
Slanting away. The wing rose up again.
They glided down on silence and the wind.

The fields were rushing at them, tilted steep.
Dodd braced himself. The glider leveled, lightly
Bumped on the ground, and rolled to a dead stop.

The door was open. They were climbing through.
And now were standing in an open field
Flat as a pancake. Gliders strewed the scene.
Others were skimming down; and still the sky
Was filled with gliders.

          From their lifted bows
The gliders were disgorging jeeps and cannon.
Riflemen formed their files and marched away.
Dodd's section took its place in the company.
The Captain raised his arm; he swept it down,
And they were marching.

On the bright horizon
A windmill stood. The land was crossed with dykes.
It looked like a Dutch painting. To their left
A wood began. They marched in that direction.

The day was hot, and Dodd began to sweat.
Then to his ears came the familiar sound
Of guns, the battle-roll, continuous.
Then all his other days were like a dream.
This was reality: the heat, the load
Strapping his shoulder, and the sound of guns.

The war, after Normandy, had seemed remote.
He had been there; his courage had been proved
To his own satisfaction. He had listened
To talk about the fighting, and he'd talked
And lost the sense of truth. He had forgotten
The smell of apples and the fear of death.
Now he remembered. And it seemed unjust
That he should be required to survive
Again. The sound increased. The battleground
Looked ominous. Visions of a huge mistake
Struck at his heart.

3

The company was entering the woods.
"Dodd," said the sergeant, "take this message up
To Lieutenant Farr."

He stepped out of the file
And hastened to the front. The lead platoon
Was walking slowly, with the scouts ahead.
He gave the message.

"Right," said the lieutenant.

The runner started back. As he went by
Faces stared into his inquiringly.
He seemed possessed of an important secret.

Shots went off behind him. He crouched and swung
Out of the path, and lay in the scrub, face down.
The firing stopped. A voice was calling "Medic!"

Fisher, a sergeant of the third platoon,
Came up the path, bent low. He shook Dodd's shoulder:
"Who's doing all the shooting?"

                    "I don't know,"
Dodd said. The sergeant, with a grim expression,
Stared at him, and went on.

                    The runner waited.
Why didn't they get it over with!

                    "Move out!"

He got to his feet. The path filled up with men.
He made his way back, past the sweating faces
Now streaked with dust. He fell in with his section,
Turned round, and traveled up the path again
He'd just traversed.

                    The files ahead were parting.
The men looked down, as into a precipice.
There was a body lying in the way.
It was Santelli, of the first platoon.
Dodd had just seen him going out in front;
He walked like a dancer, with a short, neat step,
Rifle held crosswise.

                    He lay huddled up
On his left side; his helmet had rolled off;
His head was seeping blood out in the dirt.

The files ahead were lagging; then they hurried.
"Keep your intervals!" the Captain shouted.
They hated him together.

    At the break
They sprawled out of the path, in the underbrush.
Santelli's death had made them strangely silent.
Their helmets bowed their heads down on their chests.
Under the distant thudding of the guns,
The weight of all their burdens and the sky,
They couldn't speak, or stir themselves, or lift
A cigarette.

    Dodd thought about Santelli.
One of the afternoons it seemed forever
All they would do was practice for the war
With marches, tactics, and map exercises,
He lay beneath the wall of an English garden,
Sucking a stalk of grass, and watched the clouds,
And far above the clouds, a fleet of bombers
Trailing long plumes of white across the blue.
Close by, Santelli sat, paring his nails
With a pocketknife.

    "Hey, runner-boy," he said
In the familiar and sneering tone
That Dodd despised. "What're we doin, hey?
You've been to college, right?" His little eyes
Were sharp with mockery—a little man
Of pocketknives and combs. "You ought to know.
What's it all about?"

      4

A plane flew glittering out of the sun—
A *Thunderbolt*. It swooped and disappeared

Behind a screen of trees. Then a staccato
Sound began. Machine guns. The plane rose
And flew away. They watched it till it vanished.

"On your feet," the sergeant said.

                  "My aching back!"
Someone said; but the gripe lacked conviction.
They stood and crumbled out their cigarettes,
And rolled the paper into little balls,
As though they'd like to keep the battlefield
Clean as a barracks.

           As Dodd marched, the weight
Sawed at his shoulders: pack and ammunition,
Gas mask and trench tool, bayonet, grenades.
He plodded with clenched jaws, his eyes cast down
On the dusty path, the heels moving ahead.
He stayed, it seemed, in a fixed position;
It was the scene that moved.

              The path reeled in
Another corpse. It came to him boot-first:
A German soldier on his back, spread-eagle,
A big, fresh-blooded, blond, jack-booted man
In dusty gray. Stepping around the fingers,
Around the bucket helmet, Dodd stared down.
A fly lit on the teeth. He looked away
And to the front, where other attitudes
Of death were waiting. He assumed them all,
One by one, in his imagination,
In order to prevent them.

           Small-arms fire
Was crackling through the wood. Platoons spread out
In arrow-shaped formations.

          "Dig in!"

                He dug.
The shovel sank in sand; he hacked at roots.
Overhead, shells were whispering, and smoke
Came drifting back.

               Two planes went whistling over.
Typhoons. They darted searching on the front.
They dived, and from their wings plunged rockets down
In smoking streaks. The ground shook with concussions.

"We're moving out!"

               Dodd climbed out of the hole
That he had dug. The company moved in silence
Through the burning wood.

5

Beyond the wood there stretched an open road.
They filed out on it. In a field of hay
A plane perched on its nose, a *Messerschmidt,*
The black cross glaring.

               Houses stood here and there.
In front of one, a mattress had been laid,
And on the mattress, a German officer.
He was puffed up with air like a balloon,
Belly and limbs swelling as if to split
His uniform. The grass was stuck with feathers.

Night was falling; the light had left the fields.
The road approached a village. At the entrance
A German half-track had been blown apart,
Its mustard-yellow metal torn and scorched;
Out of it spilled the crew, burned black as rubber.
The street, as they passed through, was strewn with dead,

A presentation of boot soles and teeth,
Letters, cigars, the contents of their lives.

The cannonading was more loud, and flashes
Lit the darkening sky. A company
Of paratroopers passed them, coming back
With somber faces.

6

Night. And the fields were still. The cannonade
Was flickering and grumbling through the sky.
Red flashes lined the clouds. No breath of wind
Was moving. In the holes that they had dug
The tired troops were sleeping on their arms.

"Dodd, get up!"

          He struggled out of his bag.

The First Sergeant leaned over: "Take this message
Back to Battalion."

          Dodd took the paper,
His helmet and his M-1, and set off,
Still half asleep.

          Darkness without a moon
Surrounded him. He made his lonely way
Over a road that skirted trees and dykes.
The guns were rumbling; shells went fluttering over;
Machine-gun tracers sparkled distantly.
A flare popped in the sky and glimmered down;
He waited in the shadow of a tree
Till it went out. And took the road again.

A deepening of black, a looming wall,
Was Battalion C. P. The guard called out:
"Halt! Who's there?"

                The runner spoke the password:
"Kansas!" and was admitted by the guard
Into the courtyard. There he gave his message
To a tech-sergeant; sat down on a bench,
And waited, looking at the pulsing sky.

"Runner!"

      He answered.

             "Take this message back."

That was his job. Now all I need, he thought,
Is one of those Philip Morris uniforms
The bellboys wear.

           The road was long and dark.
And it was weird to be alone in Holland
At midnight on this road. As he went on
He felt he had no weight. The landscape seemed
To have more things to think of than his journey.
These errands gave him little satisfaction.
Some men might think he led the life of Riley,
Safe and warm and dry, around Headquarters.
A man could be a runner all his life
And never be shot at. That's what they thought.
But how about the shelling? He'd been shelled
As much as anyone. And back in France,
At Carentan, he had been shot at—plenty!
It wasn't his fault he never had a chance
To fire back. Now right here on this road,
He might be killed by accident. But still,
That wouldn't be the same as being brave.

He had no chance to be thought so, no part
In the society of riflemen.
So, as he went, he reasoned with himself.

7

Next day the company went up on line
Near Veghel. They were digging round a church,
In the cemetery, and were just knee-deep
When hell broke loose.

                The screaming and flat crack
Of eighty-eights.

          Airbursts.

                 The metal slashed
The trees and ricocheted. Bit in the ground.

The runner on his belly lay contracting
Under the edge of metal. From a tree
A yard away, leaves flew. A voice cried "Medic!"

His belly and his buttocks clenched each time
A shell came in. And they kept coming in.
He felt a sting between his shoulder blades.
I'm wounded, he thought, with a rush of joy.

"Dodd!" someone called.

                He went on hands and knees
Toward the voice. "Over here," it urged him.

It was his sergeant, with a dozen cases
Of mortar shells.

"Take them up to the mortars,"
he said. "They're out of ammunition."

He took two cases, one beneath each arm,
And ran off, dodging among the trees and graves.
He found the mortars and came running back
To get another load. The crack and hum
Of the artillery was all around him.
He felt the sting of the place where he'd been hit.
He knew that he was brave.

                On the last trip,
Kneeling above a mortar, as he lowered
The cases gently, one of the mortar crew
Said, "You're a good man, Dodd."

                  That night he lay
Smiling, without a care, beneath the sky.
He had done all that could be expected.

8

October, and the sky was turning gray.
The battle line had settled. Every night
The bombers flew, going to Germany
At a great height. And back the other way
The V-1's came. The soldiers in their holes
Heard them droning and saw the rhythmic flames
Carrying woe to Antwerp and to England.

They dozed or watched. Then it began to rain,
And always rained. It seemed they were never dry.
Winter was in the air. Paths turned to mud.
By day and night the shells came shrieking in;
They got so they could tell a dying fall
And pay the rest no mind. They lived with mud.

They cooked and ate their rations in the can,
And tried to dry their socks between two rains.
Cold and sullen, under a raincoat roof,
They shivered in their holes.

One moonlit night
Dodd was returning on his way alone.
There was a wind; the haunted shadows stirred,
And rainpools glimmered in the moonlit fields.

There was a field the runner loathed to cross.
A place of horrors. Here, on the first day,
There'd been fierce charges, combats at close range,
And the dead were mixed as they had fallen.
Here crouched the German soldier with his *schmeisser*
Close to the parachutist in his rage—
Putrid things, never to be forgotten.
The field was swelling, shining with an aura
Of pale corruption.

To avoid it, Dodd
Went by another path he did not know,
Leading, it seemed, back to the company.
But in a while a fearful premonition
Stopped him. In a shadow, cold with dread,
He stood listening. The branches stirred,
And all at once there was a clash of arms,
The sounds of footsteps. Stealthily he turned
To slip away.

"*Wer geht da?*"

He ran.
He plunged into the darkness, blind with panic.
A storm of shots erupted at his back.
Brambles tore at his legs. He climbed a bank,
Clawing, and stumbled down the other side.

Then, as he ran, he shouted out the password.
"Ohio!" like a dog drenched with hot water.
His rifle fell. He left it where it was.
"Ohio!" He collided with a branch
And staggered. At his back the storm increased.
Red tracers streaked the air. Across a ditch
He leaped. And ran across the road beyond.
A hole was in his way; he cleared it with
A stride, and the dark figure starting up
Out of the hole. He kept on running, shouting
"Ohio!" A shape standing in the path
Snatched at him; he swerved out of its grasp.
There was a maze of holes. He stumbled, reeled,
And fell. His helmet flew off with a clang.

Feet were approaching. He lay still as death.
"It's Dodd," said a voice.
                              At last, he looked up
Into the faces of the third platoon.
Fisher. Others. They looked down in wonder.

9

The regiment was bivouacked near Rheims
In tents on the bare plain. Wind-driven clouds
Streamed over, and the land in chilly streaks
Heaved like a sea. The wind hummed on the ropes
And whipped the tent flaps.

                              Dodd, stretched on his cot,
Could see and hear the third platoon at drill.
They turned to the flank and to the flank again;
They marched to the rear.

                              "Count cadence . . . cadence count!"

"*Hup* . . . two . . . three . . . four!" they answered on the wind.
The sun flashed from the slanting rifle butts.

The corporal shouted: "When I say Ohio,
To the rear march, and double-time like hell!"
There was a burst of laughter, then: "Ohio!
Run!" the corporal said, "*Hup* . . . two . . . three . . . four!
Halt! Now we'll try that movement once again.
When I give the word Ohio, turn around
And double-time as if your name is Dodd.
Make it look good. All right now—forward '*arch!*
Ohio!"

          Dodd rolled over on his face.
He saw himself once more before the Captain:
"Screaming the password . . . throwing away your gun . . .
Keep out of my sight, Dodd. You make me sick."

And then, the jokes, from reveille to sleep:
"That is Ohio, one of the midwest boys."
Replacements would be sent to see Ohio
To draw their running shoes. "I'm from Cleveland,"
One of them told him. "What part are you from?"

He turned upon his back. Right overhead
His jacket hung, with regimental ribbons,
The bronze star, and his shameful purple heart.
He stared at it. If he could only sleep
The time between, until the sergeant came
To put him on another hard detail!

That was his punishment: to dig latrines,
Pick cigarette butts up, scrub greasy pots—
Or to do nothing for a live-long day
But think and try to read, in a cold tent.

When the men came in, they would ignore him—

"You going in to town?"

                 "You said it, man!"

Polishing up their paratrooper boots
Until the toes reflected a lit match;
Blousing the trousers in their boot tops; brushing
Their jackets; tucking ties between two buttons;
Cocking their caps—"Let's go!"

                         He fell asleep,
And dreamed that he was climbing. On the crest
A dummy stood, with stiff, ballooning arms
And painted face, in Prussian uniform.
He reached the arms and swung them. It went "B-r-r-r-m!"
Like a machine gun. "B-r-r-m!" the sound came out
The dummy's painted lips and barrel belly.
Then he was walking over a green field.
It was a country he had never seen,
With haystacks, a warm wind, and distant barns.
Shadows were walking with him, and a voice
Spoke with the measure of a travelogue:
"*Vingtième Division* . . . fifty per cent . . ."
Another voice inquired: "Casualties?"
"No," said the first voice, "all of them are dead."
And it continued: "*Douzième Infanterie* . . .
Fifty per cent . . ." As the first voice was speaking,
Over the field, as on a movie screen,
Hands were imposed; they held a scarlet cloth
And folded it. "René de Gaumartin,"
The voice continued, "Cardinal of France."
Again the hands were folding a red robe.
"Marcel Gaumartin, Cardinal of France."
And as the voice and the pale hands continued
Their meditative play, Dodd came upon
A girl in black. She had fair hair and skin,
Plain features, almost ugly, but her eyes
Were large, they shot out tender rays of light.

The voice said, "Mademoiselle de Maintenon."
In his dream, Dodd laughed. *De Maintenon!* She said,
In a voice remote with sadness, "Yes," and smiled,
"I try not to think of them too much."

                                     He woke,
And his heart was light. It was a vision,
He thought. What does it mean? What eyes she had!
That field, with the wind blowing, and the clouds!
And yet, it was absurd. The words were nonsense.

He went out of his tent.

                         The third platoon
Were sitting down, taking a smoking break.
"Ohio!" someone shouted. "Where you running?"

He walked the other way, toward a rise
With trees, the only trees in all the plain,
Leaving the tents behind.

                         He climbed the slope
And sat beneath a tree. On the horizon
Rheims, with the cathedral, like a ship
Traveled the plain. Clouds were streaming over
The spire; their swift shadows ran like waves.
He lit a cigarette. Then, near at hand,
He saw the earth was trenched. A long depression,
No more than a foot deep, with rotten posts
And scraps of wire, wound across the slope.
He stood, and walked along it. The earth gave
Under his boots. He picked up a small scrap
Of wire, and it crumbled. He surmised
This was a trench dug in the first Great War.
Who knew? Perhaps an older war than that.
He faced the East, to Germany and Russia.
Shadows were standing with him. It was cold.

They watched, wrapped in old overcoats, forgotten.
They stamped their feet. The whole world was deserted
Except for them; there was nobody left.
On the imagined parapet, a cross
Howled in the wind; and there were photographs
Of girls and children, bunches of cut flowers.

Then, on the pitted, gaunt escarp, the night,
The melancholy night, swept with grandeur.
Far in the dark, star shells were blossoming.
They stamped their feet. It was too cold. Too much
To expect of them. Their boots sank in the mud.
Their veins seemed ice; their jaws creaked with the cold.
They spoke, their words were carried on the wind,
Mingled, and lost.

              But now, an actual sound
Arrived distinctly. When he turned to look,
The camp was stirring; men ran to and fro.
He saw the third platoon halt in their drill,
Fall out, and run toward their tents. He moved;
He ground his cigarette out underfoot,
And hastened down the slope.

                  "Where have you been?"
Said the First Sergeant.
               "I've been for a walk.
What's going on?"
                "Full field. Ready to move
In half an hour."

           Dodd's tent was in confusion.
The men were cramming rations in their packs,
Rolling their sleeping bags, cleaning their weapons.
He labored with stiff fingers.

             Trucks drew up

Outside.

      "Get a move on!" a corporal shouted.

Dodd hitched on his pack.

              The company
Fell in and shuffled, straightening their ranks,
Eyes to the right.

        "Let's go!"

               Dodd took his place
In the line of olive drab, the overcoats,
Helmets, packs, the gloved hands holding weapons.
The roll was called; he answered to his name.

They marched up to the trucks.

             "Mount up!"

                  He climbed
Into the truck, and was packed in. The gate
Clanged shut behind him.

10

Day turned to dusk; the truck went jolting on;
The wind was drumming on the canvas hood
And prying coldly down the runner's back.
Dusk turned to evening, and the trucks behind
Were hidden. He dozed off. Monotony
Had numbed his senses like an anesthetic.
When the gears shifted he would nearly wake.
Sometimes the truck would stop for no clear reason,
And faces, blinking in their woolen caps,

Lifted and muttered; someone tried to stretch,
And this set off a ripple of complaints.
Then the truck moved again.

                        Once they dismounted,
And Dodd saw that the road wound through a forest.
There was a hill on one side; on the other,
The trees descended into a ravine.
Against that bank, a group of people stood:
Women and children dressed in country black,
With kerchiefs round their heads, and an old man
Close by a cart. The cart was piled with things:
A mattress, pots and pans. They stood in silence
Watching the soldiers. Then the trucks reloaded,
And the onlookers vanished.

                        They were driving
More slowly now. The men were all awake.
Another stop. Again the tailgate opened,
And they dismounted.

                        This, then, was the place.
Colliding in the dark, they formed platoons,
And marched away.

                        A signpost read *Bastogne.*
They marched through a dark village with locked doors,
And were led off the road, into the woods.
The path was very dark, the march confused,
With frequent halts.

                        They halted in one place
Endlessly; they reclined, propped on their packs.
His helmet dragged Dodd's head back on his neck;
His feet got cold; under his woolen shirt
The sweat was trickling, then began to chill.

Then they were roused, pressed on without a pause,
Till, on a ridge commanding a black slope,
They halted. And the order came: "Dig in!"

Dodd unhitched his pack, laid it on the ground,
And leaned his rifle on it. From his belt
He took his trench tool out, and opened it.
He stuck the shovel blade into the ground
And levered it. He'd barely circumscribed
A foxhole, when a cold chill touched his cheek—
Snow!

That's all we needed, the runner said
To the malignant sky.

From branch to branch
Snow glimmered down and speckled the dim ground.
Dodd dragged a fallen branch across his hole
And made a roof.

"Pack up," the sergeant said.
"We're moving out."

God help them, they were led
By officers and morons, who had orders
For wearing leather out and breaking spades,
To give employment to the men at home
Who, on this freezing night, were warm in bed
With soldiers' wives!

Having said so, they walked
On in the stumbling dark, till once again
They halted, in a place just like the first.

"Dig in!"

And it was useless, but they dug

With the energy of a supreme contempt
Marvelous holes—each clammy wedge of earth
An accusation flung in heaven's face.

Then, like a sound engendered by their mood,
An angry muttering rose on the night.
It faded, and again came to their ears—
The sound of guns.

                  At last, Dodd's hole was finished.
He lowered himself, rolled out his sleeping bag,
And pushed into it. Flickerings of light
Twitched overhead; the guns were coming closer.
Here, it was still. The snow came drifting down.

"Dodd, you're on guard."

                      He climbed out of his hole.

"There, by the trees."

                  He walked across the snow,
And as he went he looked around, astonished—
The sky was lit with spots of burning red
In a great circle.

                As he stood on guard,
Surveying the black slope, the distant fires,
A man approached. Dodd challenged him. He spoke
The password, and came slogging through the trees.
A runner from Battalion. Brushing snow
Out of his neck, he asked for the C. P.
Dodd pointed: "Over there. Close to the barn.
What's happening now?"

                "We're up a creek, that's what!
They're coming—panzers from the Russians front,

Under Von Runstedt. Panzers and SS.
I was just talking to a man who said
The line at St. Vith has been overrun
By tanks. It was a total massacre.
They're dropping paratroopers too," he said,
And turned away. He paused again to add:
"Everyone else is pulling out but us,"
And trudged away, leaving Dodd to his thoughts.

11

The night was long. And day seemed less to rise
Than darkness to withdraw. Dodd, in his hole,
Could hear the fire of small arms, that seems
More threatening to the solitary man
Than does artillery.

                One hole away
A helmet like a turtle shell was stirring.
A puffy face with whiskers turned around;
It was the mailman, Lopez. He arranged
Twigs on the snow. On these, his drinking mug.
He struck a match, applied it to the twigs,
And nursed the flame with cupped hands, bending over.

Under the hanging sky, congealed with clouds,
Fog trailed and clung to the earth; and the Ardennes,
The spectral firs, their branches cloaked with snow,
Stood stark against the foggy atmosphere.

Dodd stamped his feet. He stooped, and from his pack
Took a K-ration box. He tore it open,
Shook out the can of egg, the pack of biscuits,
The packet of coffee. He removed a glove
And with that hand put snow into his mug.
Poured coffee in, and mixed it with his spoon.

He scooped a hollow in the snow, and piled
Some twigs in it, and strips of the ration box.
And then put the mug on, and lit the pile.

Voices came floating up—loud gutturals;
A whine and clanking of machinery.
He picked his gun up.

                    At the foot of the slope
The trees were shaking, parting. There emerged
A cannon barrel with a muzzle brake.
It slid out like a snake's head, slowly swinging.
It paused. A flash of light came from its head;
A thunder clap exploded to Dodd's left;
Metal whanged on the slope, a spume of black
Hung in the air.

                    Then, endlessly it seemed,
The barrel slid out. With a thrash of branches
A tank appeared. It lurched, seemed to consider,
And then came on, at an appalling rate.
The engine whined; the tracks jingled and squeaked.
And imperceptibly, out of the trees
Stood men, like apparitions of the snow.

And now it was a swarm of walking men
In field-gray and in white, with capes and hoods.

Dodd placed his elbows on the snow, took aim—
There was another thunder clap. He ducked
And came upright again. To left and right
Rifles were firing. Hastily he pointed
The muzzle at a running, hooded shape,
And pressed the trigger. As in a nightmare
Nothing happened. A bullet cracked by his head.
The safety catch was on. He pressed it—forward,
And aimed the gun again, and squeezed the trigger.

The butt kicked in his shoulder, the brass jumped
Into the snow.

                    The tank was growing large.
The cannon flashed. Machine-gun tracers curved
Toward it, and played sparkling on the steel.
Still it came on, glittering in return
From its machine guns. Then, a crashing flame
Struck it, leaving a trail of smoke in air.
The tank shuddered. It slewed broadside around.
Inside the plates, as on an anvil, hammers
Were laboring. It trembled with explosions,
And smoke poured out of it.

                         The slope was still,
Sprawling with hooded figures—and the rest
Gone back into the trees. Then there began
The sound of the wounded.

                              Dodd stood up
And looked around. In the next hole, a helmet
Moved cautiously.

                    "Lopez," he inquired,
"Are you all right?"

                    "Jesus!" the mailman said.

With a shaking hand, Dodd felt for cigarettes.
He breathed tobacco deep into his lungs.
On the twigs where he had left it balanced
His mug was hissing and—he held it—warm.

                    12

Sometimes the snow came drifting down again.
And when it ceased, eddies and gusts of wind

Would lift it in long skirts that swept across
The dead. It packed into the stiffened folds
Of clothing. When night fell, a freezing wind
Encased the tree trunks in bright sheaths of ice
And hung bright icicles on every branch,
And clamped the dead in rigid attitudes.

A shell came whistling down. The runner clenched
His fists. It crashed. Another shell came in.
The crashes jarred the ground. Then, from the rear,
A battery replied; shells fluttered back.

"Dodd!"

      He unzipped his bag, put on his helmet,
And stood.

        "Where are you?"

          It was the First Sergeant.

"Here," the runner answered.

        "Take this message
Back to Battalion. Are you listening?"

"Yes," he said.

        "To Colonel Jesserman.
The Captain says we need a fifty-seven
Or tank-destroyer. Tell him that it's urgent.
Now you repeat the message."

        Dodd did so.
He slung his rifle over his right shoulder
And climbed out of his hole.

                    "Keep out of trouble,"
The sergeant said. "Don't stop for anything."
Dodd started to move off. The sergeant grasped
His arm: "Watch out! They may have got patrols
Between us and Battalion. Good luck!"

Dodd waved his hand, although it was too dark
For the other to see him. And set off
In what seemed to be the right direction.

                              Rome. December 2, 1957

The Bird

"*Ich wünscht', ich wäre ein Vöglein*,"
Sang Heinrich, "I would fly
Across the sea. . . ." so sadly
It made his mother cry.

At night he played his zither,
By day worked in the mine.
His friend was Hans; together
The boys walked by the Rhine.

"Each day we're growing older,"
Hans said, "this is no life.
I wish I were a soldier!"
And snapped his pocketknife.

War came, and Hans was taken,
But Heinrich did not fight.
"*Ich wünscht', ich wäre ein Vöglein*,"
Sang Heinrich every night.

"Dear Heinrich," said the letter,
"I hope this finds you fine.
The war could not be better,
It's women, song, and wine."

A letter came for Heinrich,
The same that he'd sent east
To Hans, his own handwriting
Returned, and marked *Deceased*.

*

"You'll never be a beauty,"
The doctor said, "you scamp!
We'll give you special duty,
A concentration camp."

And now the truck was nearing
The place. They passed a house;
A radio was blaring
The *Wiener Blut* of Strauss.

The banks were bright with flowers,
The birds sang in the wood;
There was a fence with towers
On which armed sentries stood.

They stopped. The men dismounted;
Heinrich got down—at last!
"That chimney," said the sergeant,
"That's where the Jews are gassed."

*

Each day he sorted clothing,
Skirt, trousers, boot, and shoe,
Till he was filled with loathing
For every size of Jew.

"Come in! What is it, Private?"
"Please Sir, that vacancy.
I wonder, could I have it?"
"Your papers! Let me see.

You're steady and you're sober,
But have you learned to kill?"
Said Heinrich, "No, *Herr Ober-
Leutnant,* but I will!"

"The Reich can use your spirit.
Report to Unit Four.
Here is an armband—wear it!
Dismissed! Don't slam the door."

*

"Ich wünscht', ich wäre ein Vöglein,"
Sang Heinrich, "I would fly . . ."
They knew that when they heard him
The next day they would die.

They stood in silence praying
At midnight when they heard
The zither softly playing,
The singing of the Bird.

He stared into the fire,
He sipped a glass of wine.
"Ich wünscht'," his voice rose higher,
"Ich wäre ein Vöglein."

A dog howled in its kennel,
He thought of Hans and cried.
The stars looked down from heaven.
That day the children died.

*

"The Russian tanks are coming!"
The wind bore from the East
A cannonade, a drumming
Of small arms that increased.

Heinrich went to Headquarters.
He found the Colonel dead

With pictures of his daughters,
A pistol by his head.

He thought, his courage sinking,
"There's always the SS. . . ."
He found the Major drinking
In a woman's party dress.

The prisoners were shaking
Their barracks. Heinrich heard
A sound of timber breaking,
A shout, "Where is the Bird?"

*

The Russian was completing
A seven-page report.
He wrote: "We still are beating
The woods. . . ." Then he stopped short.

A little bird was flitting
Outside, from tree to tree.
He turned where he was sitting
And watched it thoughtfully.

He pulled himself together,
And wrote: "We've left no stone
Unturned—but not a feather!
It seems the Bird has flown.

Description? Half a dozen
Group snapshots, badly blurred;
And which is Emma's cousin
God knows, and which the Bird!

He could be in the Western
Or in the Eastern Zone.

I'd welcome a suggestion
If anything is known."

*

"*Ich wünscht', ich wäre ein Vöglein,*"
Sings Heinrich, "I would fly
Across the sea. . . ." so sadly
It makes his children cry.

The Silent Generation

When Hitler was the Devil
He did as he had sworn
With such enthusiasm
That even, *donnerwetter,*
The Germans say, "Far better
Had he been never born!"

It was my generation
That put the Devil down
With great enthusiasm.
But now our occupation
Is gone. Our education
Is wasted on the town.

We lack enthusiasm.
Life seems a mystery;
It's like the play a lady
Told me about: "It's not . . .
It doesn't *have* a plot,"
She said. "It's history."

The Lover's Ghost

I fear the headless man
Whose military scars
Proclaim his merit.
And yet I fear a woman
More than the ghost of Mars,
A wounded spirit.

That look, all kindness lost,
Cold hands, as cold as stone,
A wanton gesture
"What do you want, old ghost?
How long must I atone?"
So I addressed her.

"Did you not call?" she said.
"Goodbye, then! For I go
Where I am wanted."
Till dawn I tossed in bed
Wishing that I could know
Who else she haunted.

The Goodnight

He stood still by her bed
Watching his daughter breathe,
The dark and silver head,
The fingers curled beneath,
And thought: Though she may have
Intelligence and charm
And luck, they will not save
Her life from every harm.

The lives of children are
Dangerous to their parents
With fire, water, air,
And other accidents;
And some, for a child's sake,
Anticipating doom,
Empty the world to make
The world safe as a room.

Who could endure the pain
That was Laocoon's?
Twisting, he saw again
In the same coil his sons.
Plumed in his father's skill,
Young Icarus flew higher
Toward the sun, until
He fell in rings of fire.

A man who cannot stand
Children's perilous play,
With lifted voice and hand
Drives the children away.
Out of sight, out of reach,
The tumbling children pass;

He sits on an empty beach,
Holding an empty glass.

Who said that tenderness
Will turn the heart to stone?
May I endure her weakness
As I endure my own.
Better to say goodnight
To breathing flesh and blood
Each night as though the night
Were always only good.

from
AT THE END OF THE OPEN ROAD

1963
✻

In California

Here I am, troubling the dream coast
With my New York face,
Bearing among the realtors
And tennis players my dark preoccupation.

There once was an epical clatter—
Voices and banjos, Tennessee, Ohio,
Rising like incense in the sight of heaven.
Today, there is an angel in the gate.

Lie back, Walt Whitman,
There, on the fabulous raft with the King and the Duke!
For the white row of the Marina
Faces the Rock. Turn round the wagons here.

Lie back! We cannot bear
The stars any more, those infinite spaces.
Let the realtors divide the mountain,
For they have already subdivided the valley.

Rectangular city blocks astonished
Herodotus in Babylon,
Cortez in Tenochtitlan,
And here's the same old city-planner, death.

We cannot turn or stay.
For though we sleep, and let the reins fall slack,
The great cloud-wagons move
Outward still, dreaming of a Pacific.

In the Suburbs

There's no way out.
You were born to waste your life.
You were born to this middleclass life

As others before you
Were born to walk in procession
To the temple, singing.

The Redwoods

Mountains are moving, rivers
are hurrying. But we
are still.

We have the thoughts of giants—
clouds, and at night the stars.

And we have names—guttural, grotesque—
Hamet, Og—names with no syllables.

And perish, one by one, our roots
gnawed by the mice. And fall.

And are too slow for death, and change
to stone. Or else too quick,

like candles in a fire. Giants
are lonely. We have waited long

for someone. By our waiting, surely
there must be someone at whose touch

our boughs would bend; and hands
to gather us; a spirit

to whom we are light as the hawthorn tree.
O if there is a poet

let him come now! We stand at the Pacific
like great unmarried girls,

turning in our heads the stars and clouds,
considering whom to please.

There Is

Look! From my window there's a view
of city streets
where only lives as dry as tortoises
can crawl—the Gallapagos of desire.

There is the day of Negroes with red hair
and the day of insane women on the subway;
there is the day of the word Trieste
and the night of the blind man with the electric guitar.

But I have no profession. Like a spy
I read the papers—Situations Wanted.
Surely there is a secret
which, if I knew it, would change everything!

*

I have the poor man's nerve-tic, irony.
I see through the illusions of the age!
The bell tolls, and the hearse advances,
and the mourners follow, for my entertainment.

I tread the burning pavement,
the streets where drunkards stretch
like photographs of civil death
and trumpets strangle in electric shelves.

The mannequins stare at me scornfully.
I know they are pretending
all day to be in earnest.
And can it be that love is an illusion?

When darkness falls on the enormous street
the air is filled with Eros, whispering.

Eyes, mouths, contrive to meet
in silence, fearing they may be prevented.

       *

O businessmen like ruins,
bankers who are Bastilles,
widows, sadder than the shores of lakes,
then you were happy, when you still could tremble!

But all night long my window
sheds tears of light.
I seek the word. The word is not forthcoming.
O syllables of light . . . O dark cathedral . . .

Summer Morning

There are whole blocks in New York
Where no one lives—
A district of small factories.
And there's a hotel; one morning

When I was there with a girl
We saw in the window opposite
Men and women working at their machines.
Now and then one looked up.

Toys, hardware—whatever they made,
It's been worn out.
I'm fifteen years older myself—
Bad years and good.

So I have spoiled my chances.
For what? Sheer laziness,
The thrill of an assignation,
My life that I hold in secret.

Birch

Birch tree, you remind me
Of a room filled with breathing,
The sway and whisper of love.

She slips off her shoes;
Unzips her skirt; arms raised,
Unclasps an earring, and the other.

Just so the sallow trunk
Divides, and the branches
Are pale and smooth.

The Morning Light

In the morning light a line
Stretches forever. There my unlived life
Rises, and I resist,
Clinging to the steps of the throne.

Day lifts the darkness from the hills,
A bright blade cuts the reeds,
And my life, pitilessly demanding,
Rises forever in the morning light.

The Cradle Trap

A bell and rattle,
a smell of roses,
a leather Bible,
and angry voices.

They say, I love you.
They shout, You must!
The light is telling
terrible stories.

But night at the window
whispers, Never mind.
Be true, be true
to your own strange kind.

A Story About Chicken Soup

In my grandmother's house there was always chicken soup
And talk of the old country—mud and boards,
Poverty,
The snow falling down the necks of lovers.

Now and then, out of her savings
She sent them a dowry. Imagine
The rice-powdered faces!
And the smell of the bride, like chicken soup.

But the Germans killed them.
I know it's in bad taste to say it,
But it's true. The Germans killed them all.

                    *

In the ruins of Berchtesgaden
A child with yellow hair
Ran out of a doorway.

A German girl-child—
Cuckoo, all skin and bones—
Not even enough to make chicken soup.
She sat by the stream and smiled.

Then as we splashed in the sun
She laughed at us.
We had killed her mechanical brothers,
So we forgave her.

                    *

The sun is shining.
The shadows of the lovers have disappeared.

They are all eyes; they have some demand on me—
They want me to be more serious than I want to be.

They want me to stick in their mudhole
Where no one is elegant.
They want me to wear old clothes,
They want me to be poor, to sleep in a room with many others—

Not to walk in the painted sunshine
To a summer house,
But to live in the tragic world forever.

The Troika

Troika, troika! The snow moon
whirls through the forest.

Where lamplight like a knife
gleams through a door, I see two graybeards bending.
They're playing chess, it seems. And then one rises
and stands in silence. Does he hear me passing?

Troika, troika! In the moonlight
his spirit hears my spirit passing.

I whip the horses on. The houses vanish.
The moon looks over fields
littered with debris. And there in trenches
the guardsmen stand, wind fluttering their rags.

And there were darker fields without a moon.
I walk across a field, bound on an errand.
The errand's forgotten—something depended on it.
A nightmare! I have lost my father's horses!

And then a white bird rises
and goes before me, hopping through the forest.

I held the bird—it vanished with a cry,
and on a branch a girl sat sideways, combing
her long black hair. The dew
shone on her lips; her breasts were white as roses.

Troika, troika! Three white horses,
a whip of silver, and my father's sleigh . . .

When morning breaks, the sea
gleams through the branches,
and the white bird, enchanted,
is flying through the world, across the sea.

Frogs

The storm broke, and it rained,
And water rose in the pool,
And frogs hopped into the gutter,

With their skins of yellow and green,
And just their eyes shining above the surface
Of the warm solution of slime.

At night, when fireflies trace
Light-lines between the trees and flowers
Exhaling perfume,

The frogs speak to each other
In rhythm. The sound is monstrous,
But their voices are filled with satisfaction.

In the city I pine for the country;
In the country I long for conversation—
Our happy croaking.

My Father in the Night Commanding No

My father in the night commanding No
Has work to do. Smoke issues from his lips;
    He reads in silence.
The frogs are croaking and the street lamps glow.

And then my mother winds the gramophone,
The Bride of Lammermoor begins to shriek—
    Or reads a story
About a prince, a castle, and a dragon.

The moon is glittering above the hill.
I stand before the gateposts of the King—
    So runs the story—
Of Thule, at midnight when the mice are still.

And I have been in Thule! It has come true—
The journey and the danger of the world,
    All that there is
To bear and to enjoy, endure and do.

Landscapes, seascapes . . . where have I been led?
The names of cities—Paris, Venice, Rome—
    Held out their arms.
A feathered god, seductive, went ahead.

Here is my house. Under a red rose tree
A child is swinging; another gravely plays.
    They are not surprised
That I am here; they were expecting me.

And yet my father sits and reads in silence,
My mother sheds a tear, the moon is still,
    And the dark wind
Is murmuring that nothing ever happens.

Beyond his jurisdiction as I move
Do I not prove him wrong? And yet, it's true
    They will not change
There, on the stage of terror and of love.

The actors in that playhouse always sit
In fixed positions—father, mother, child
    With painted eyes.
How sad it is to be a little puppet!

Their heads are wooden. And you once pretended
To understand them! Shake them as you will,
    They cannot speak.
Do what you will, the comedy is ended.

Father, why did you work? Why did you weep,
Mother? Was the story so important?
    "Listen!" the wind
Said to the children, and they fell asleep.

American Poetry

Whatever it is, it must have
A stomach that can digest
Rubber, coal, uranium, moons, poems.

Like the shark it contains a shoe.
It must swim for miles through the desert
Uttering cries that are almost human.

The Inner Part

When they had won the war
And for the first time in history
Americans were the most important people—

When the leading citizens no longer lived in their shirt sleeves
And their wives did not scratch in public;
Just when they'd stopped saying "Gosh!"—

When their daughters seemed as sensitive
As the tip of a fly rod,
And their sons were as smooth as a V-8 engine—

Priests, examining the entrails of birds,
Found the heart misplaced, and seeds
As black as death, emitting a strange odor.

On the Lawn at the Villa

On the lawn at the villa—
That's the way to start, eh, reader?
We know where we stand—somewhere expensive—
You and I *imperturbes,* as Walt would say,
Before the diversions of wealth, you and I *engagés.*

On the lawn at the villa
Sat a manufacturer of explosives,
His wife from Paris,
And a young man named Bruno,

And myself, being American,
Willing to talk to these malefactors,
The manufacturer of explosives, and so on,
But somehow superior. By that I mean democratic.
It's complicated, being an American,
Having the money and the bad conscience, both at the same time.
Perhaps, after all, this is not the right subject for a poem.

We were all sitting there paralyzed
In the hot Tuscan afternoon,
And the bodies of the machine-gun crew were draped over the
        balcony.
So we sat there all afternoon.

The Riders Held Back

One morning as we traveled in the fields
    Of air and dew
With trumpets, and above the painted shields
    The banners flew,

We came upon three ladies, wreathed in roses,
    Where, hand in hand,
They danced—three slender, gentle, naked ladies
    All in a woodland.

They'd been to the best schools in Italy,
    Their legs were Greek,
Their collarbones, as fine as jewelry,
    Their eyes, antique.

"Why do lambs skip and shepherds shout 'Ut hoy!'?
    Why do you dance?"
Said one, "It is an intellectual joy,
    The Renaissance.

"As do the stars in heaven, ruled by Three,
    We twine and move.
It is the music of Astronomy,
    Not men, we love.

"And as we dance, the beasts and flowers do;
    The fields of wheat
Sway like our arms; the curving hills continue
    The curves of our feet.

"Here Raphael comes to paint; the thrushes flute
    To Petrarch's pen.
But Michael is not here, who carved the brute
    Unfinished men."

They danced again, and on the mountain heights
    There seemed to rise
Towers and ramparts glittering with lights,
    Like Paradise.

How the bright morning passed, I cannot say,
    We woke and found
The dancers gone, and heard, far, far away
    The trumpet sound.

We galloped to it. In the forest then
    Banners and shields
Were strewn like leaves; and there were many slain
    In the dark fields.

Wind, Clouds, and the Delicate Curve of the World

Wind, clouds, and the delicate curve of the world
Stretching so far away . . .
On a cloud in the clear sight of heaven
Sit Kali and Jesus, disputing.
Tree shadows, cloud shadows
Falling across the body of the world
That sleeps with one arm thrown across her eyes . . .
A wind stirs in the daisies
And trees are sighing,
"These houses and these gardens are illusions."
Leaf shadows, cloud shadows,
And the wind moving as far as the eye can reach . . .

Walt Whitman at Bear Mountain

. . . life which does not give the preference to any other life, of any
previous period, which therefore prefers its own existence . . .
                    ORTEGA Y GASSET

Neither on horseback nor seated,
But like himself, squarely on two feet,
The poet of death and lilacs
Loafs by the footpath. Even the bronze looks alive
Where it is folded like cloth. And he seems friendly.

"Where is the Mississippi panorama
And the girl who played the piano?
Where are you, Walt?
The Open Road goes to the used-car lot.

"Where is the nation you promised?
These houses built of wood sustain
Colossal snows,
And the light above the street is sick to death.

"As for the people—see how they neglect you!
Only a poet pauses to read the inscription."

"I am here," he answered.
"It seems you have found me out.
Yet did I not warn you that it was Myself
I advertised? Were my words not sufficiently plain?

"I gave no prescriptions,
And those who have taken my moods for prophecies
Mistake the matter."
Then, vastly amused—"Why do you reproach me?
I freely confess I am wholly disreputable.
Yet I am happy, because you have found me out."

A crocodile in wrinkled metal loafing . . .

Then all the realtors,
Pickpockets, salesmen and the actors performing
Official scenarios,
Turned a deaf ear, for they had contracted
American dreams.

But the man who keeps a store on a lonely road,
And the housewife who knows she's dumb,
And the earth, are relieved.

All that grave weight of America
Cancelled! Like Greece and Rome.
The future in ruins!
The castles, the prisons, the cathedrals
Unbuilding, and roses
Blossoming from the stones that are not there . . .

The clouds are lifting from the high Sierras,
The Bay mists clearing,
And the angel in the gate, the flowering plum,
Dances like Italy, imagining red.

from
SELECTED POEMS

1965
✳

Stumpfoot on 42nd Street

1

A Negro sprouts from the pavement like an asparagus.
One hand beats a drum and cymbal;
He plays a trumpet with the other.

He flies the American flag;
When he goes walking, from stump to stump,
It twitches, and swoops, and flaps.

Also, he has a tin cup which he rattles;
He shoves it right in your face.
These freaks are alive in earnest.

He is not embarrassed.
It is for you to feel embarrassed,
Or God, or the way things are.

Therefore he plays the trumpet
And therefore he beats the drum.

2

I can see myself in Venezuela,
With flowers, and clouds in the distance.
The mind tends to drift.

But Stumpfoot stands near a window
Advertising cameras, trusses, household utensils.
The billboards twinkle. The time
Is 12:26.

O why don't angels speak in the infinite
To each other? Why this confusion,
These particular bodies—
Eros with clenched fists, sobbing and cursing?

The time is 12:26,
The streets lead on in burning lines
And giants tremble in electric chains.

3

I can see myself in the middle of Venezuela
Stepping in a nest of ants.
I can see myself being eaten by ants.

My ribs are caught in a thorn bush
And thought has no reality.
But he has furnished his room

With a chair and table.
A chair is like a dog, it waits for man.
He unstraps his apparatus,

And now he is taking off his boots.
He is easing his stumps,
And now he is lighting a cigar.

It seems that a man exists
Only to say, Here I am in person.

After Midnight

The dark streets are deserted,
With only a drugstore glowing
Softly, like a sleeping body;

With one white, naked bulb
In the back, that shines
On suicides and abortions.

Who lives in these dark houses?
I am suddenly aware
I might live here myself.

The garage man returns
And puts the change in my hand,
Counting the singles carefully.

from
ADVENTURES OF THE LETTER I

1971
✳

Dvonya

In the town of Odessa
there is a garden
and Dvonya is there,
Dvonya whom I love
though I have never been in Odessa.

I love her black hair, and eyes
as green as a salad
that you gather in August
between the roots of alder,
her skin with an odor of wildflowers.

We understand each other perfectly.
We are cousins twice removed.
In the garden we drink our tea,
discussing the plays of Chekhov
as evening falls and the lights begin to twinkle.

But this is only a dream.
I am not there
with my citified speech,
and the old woman is not there
peering between the curtains.

We are only phantoms, bits of ash,
like yesterday's newspaper
or the smoke of chimneys.
All that passed long ago
on a summer night in Odessa.

A Son of the Romanovs

This is Avram the cello-mender,
the only Jewish sergeant
in the army of the Tsar.
One day he was mending cellos
when they shouted, "The Tsar is coming,
everyone out or inspection!"
When the Tsar saw Avram marching
with Russians who were seven feet tall,
he said, "He must be a genius.
I want that fellow at headquarters."

Luck is given by God.
A wife you must find for yourself.

So Avram married a rich widow
who lived in a house in Odessa.
The place was filled with music.
Yasnaya Polyana with noodles.

One night in the middle of a concert
they heard a knock at the door.
So Avram went. It was a beggar,
a Russian, who had been blessed
by God—that is, he was crazy.
And he said, "I'm a natural son
of the Grand Duke Nicholas."

And Avram said, "Eat.
I owe your people a favor."
And he said, "My wife is complaining
we need someone to open the door."
So Nicholas stayed with them for years.
Who ever head of Jewish people
with a footman?

And then the Germans came. Imagine
the scene—the old people
holding onto their baggage,
and the children—they've been told it's a game,
but they don't believe it.

Then the German says, "Who's this?"
pointing at Nicholas,
"He doesn't look like a Jew."
And he said, "I'm the natural son
of the Grand Duke Nicholas."
And they saw he was feeble-minded,
and took him away too, to the death chamber.

"He could have kept his mouth shut,"
said my Grandmother,
"but what can you expect.
All of those Romanovs were a little bit crazy."

Meyer

In Russia there were three students,
Chaim, Baruch, and Meyer.
"As Maimonides says," said Meyer.
"Speaking of the Flood," said Baruch.
"*Etsev,*" said Chaim, "an equivocal term."

In spring when the birch trees shine like crystal
and the light is so clear that a butterfly
makes dark strokes in the air,
there came three students of Hebrew
and the girls from the button factory—

Dvoira, Malka, Rifkele . . .
a mystery, a fragrance,
and a torment to the scholars.
They couldn't have kept a goat, for the milk,
much less the fastidious girls of our province.

*

One night, the red star rising,
a beautiful dream came to Meyer,
a *moujik* who gave him a kiss,
and he heard a voice say, "Meyer,
and Lermontov, and Pushkin."

Dark roofs of Volhynia,
do you remember Meyer
who went to the University
and later he joined the Communist Party?
Last night I dreamed of Meyer . . .

He turned his head and smiled.

With his hand he made a sign . . .
then his features changed, he was mournful,
and I heard him say in a clear voice,
"Beware! These men killed Meyer."

The Country House

You always know what to expect
in a novel by L. V. Kalinin. . . .

"One morning in June,
in the provincial town of X,
had you been observant,
you might have seen a stranger
alighting at the railroad station."

From there it moves to a country house,
introduction of the principal characters—
a beautiful girl, a youth
on fire with radical ideas.

There are drawing-room discussions,
picnics at the lake, or a mountain,
if there is one in the vicinity.

Then some misunderstanding—
the young man banished from the house
by the angry father. Tears.

All this with the most meticulous attention
to the "spirit of the times,"
bearing in mind the classical saying,
"Don't be the first to try anything, or the last."

*

The tone of his letters was quite different:

'The Polish girl I told you about, who is living with us,
has a wart. Two days ago, the idiot

tried to remove it with lye.
For hours on end the house has been filled with howling,
and I can't think or write."

A Night in Odessa

Grandfather puts down his tea glass
and makes his excuses
and sets off, taking his umbrella.
The street lamps shine through a fog
and drunkards reel on the pavement.

One man clenches his fists in anger,
another utters terrible sobs. . . .
And women look on calmly.
They like those passionate sounds.
He walks on, grasping his umbrella.

His path lies near the forest.
Suddenly a wolf leaps in the path,
jaws dripping. The man strikes
with the point of his umbrella. . . .
A howl, and the wolf has vanished.

Go on, grandfather, hop!
It takes brains to live here,
not to be beaten and torn
or to lie drunk in a ditch.
Hold on to your umbrella!

He's home. When he opens the door
his wife jumps up to greet him.
Her name is Ninotchka,
she is young and dark and slender,
married only a month or so.

She hurries to get his supper.
But when she puts down the dish

she presses a hand to her side
and he sees that from her hand
red drops of blood are falling.

Isidor

Isidor was always plotting
to overthrow the government.
The family lived in one room. . . .
A window rattles, a woman coughs,
snow drifts over the rooftops . . .
despair. An intelligent household.

One day, there's a knock at the door. . . .
The police! A confusion . . .
Isidor's wife throws herself
on the mattress . . . she groans
as though she is in labor.
The police search everywhere,
and leave. Then a leg comes out . . .
an arm . . . then a head with spectacles.
Isidor was under the mattress!

When I think about my family
I have a feeling of suffocation.
Next time . . . how about the oven?

The mourners are sitting around
weeping and tearing their clothes.
The inspector comes. He looks in the oven . . .
there's Isidor, with his eyes
shut fast . . . his hands are folded.
The inspector nods, and goes.
Then a leg comes out, and the other.
Isidor leaps, he dances . . .

"Praise God, may His Name be exalted!"

Indian Country

1
The Shadow-Hunter

This prairie light . . . I see
a warrior and a child.

The man points, and the child
runs after a butterfly.

Rising and floating in the windy field,
that's how they learned to run . . .

Plenty Coups,
Red Cloud, Coyote, Pine Marten.

Now I will lie down in the grass
that Plenty Coups loved.

There are voices in the wind, strong voices
in the tenderness of these leaves,

and the deer move with the shade
into the hills I dream of.

There the young men live by hunting
the shadows of ideas,

and at night they march no further.
Their tents shine in the moonlight.

2
Black Kettle Raises the Stars and Stripes

"Nits make lice," said Chivington.
"Kill the nits and you'll get no lice."

The white men burst in at sunrise, shooting and stabbing.
And there was old Black Kettle
tying the Stars and Stripes to his tent pole,
and the squaws running in every direction

around Sand Creek,
a swept corner of the American consciousness.

And it's no use playing the tuba to a dead Indian.

3
On the Prairie

The wind in the leaves makes a sound
like clear running water.

I can smell the store where harness used to be sold. . . .
Morning of little leaves,

morning of cool, clear sunlight,
when the house stirred with the earnestness

of the life they really had . . .
morning with a clang of machinery.

Now an old man sits on the porch;
I can hear it every time he clears his throat . . .

as I stand here, holding the jack,
in the middle of my generation,

by the Lethe of asphalt and dust
and human blood spilled carelessly.

When I look back I see
a field full of grasshoppers.

The hills are hidden with a cloud.
And what pale king sits in the glass?

The Climate of Paradise

A story about Indians,
the tribe that claimed Mt. Shasta . . .

Five lawyers said, "It's ridiculous!
What possible use can they have for the mountain?"

The interpreter said, "Your Honor,
they say that their gods live there."

        *

How different this is from the Buzzy Schofields,
people I met in Pasadena.

Green lawns, imposing villas—
actually, these are caves inhabited

by Pufendorf's dwarfs and Vico's
Big Feet, the "abandoned by God."

Thought, says Vico, begins in caves—
but not the Buzzy Schofields'.

They're haunted by Red China—
bugles—a sky lit with artillery.

They're terrified they'll be brainwashed.
They can see themselves breaking under torture. . . .

"Stop! I'm on your side!
You're making a terrible mistake!"

O even in Paradise
the mind would make its own winter.

American Dreams

In dreams my life came toward me,
my loves that were slender as gazelles.
But America also dreams. . . .
Dream, you are flying over Russia,
dream, you are falling in Asia.

As I look down the street
on a typical sunny day in California
it is my house that is burning
and my dear ones that lie in the gutter
as the American army enters.

Every day I wake far away
from my life, in a foreign country.
These people are speaking a strange language.
It is strange to me
and strange, I think, even to themselves.

The Photographer

A bearded man seated on a camp-stool—
"The Geologist. 1910."

"Staying with Friends"—a boy in a straw hat,
on a porch, surrounded with wisteria.

"Noontime"—a view of the Battery
with masts passing over the rooftops.

Then the old horse-cars on Broadway,
people standing around in the garment district.

A high view of Manhattan,
light-shelves with sweeps of shadow.

"Jumpers"—as they come plunging down
their hair bursts into fire.

Then there are photographs of a door knob,
a chair, an unstrung tennis racket.

"Still life. Yes, for a while.
It gives your ideas a connection.

And a beautiful woman yawning
with the back of her hand, like this."

Vandergast and the Girl

Vandergast to his neighbors—
the grinding of a garage door
and hiss of gravel in the driveway.

He worked for the insurance company
whose talisman is a phoenix
rising in flames . . . *non omnis moriar.*
From his desk he had a view of the street—

translucent raincoats, and umbrellas,
fluorescent plate-glass windows.
A girl knelt down, arranging
underwear on a female dummy—

sea waves and, on the gale,
Venus, these busy days,
poised in her garter belt and stockings.

                    *

The next day he saw her eating
in the restaurant where he usually ate.

Soon they were having lunch together
elsewhere.

          She came from Dallas.
This was only a start, she was ambitious,
twenty-five and still unmarried.
Green eyes with silver filaments . . .
red hair . . .

          When he held the car door open
her legs were smooth and slender.

"I was wondering,"
she said, "when you'd get round to it,"
and laughed.

                        *

Vandergast says he never intended
having an affair.

                And was that what this was?
The names that people give to things . . .
What do definitions and divorce-court proceedings
have to do with the breathless reality?

O little lamp at the bedside
with views of Venice and the Bay of Naples,
you understood! *Lactona* toothbrush
and suitcase bought in a hurry,
you were the witnesses of the love
we made in bed together.

Schrafft's Chocolate Cherries, surely you remember
when she said she'd be true forever,

and, watching "Dark Storm," we decided
there is something to be said, after all,
for soap opera, "if it makes people happy."

                        *

The Vandergasts are having some trouble
finding a buyer for their house.

When I go for a walk with Tippy
I pass the unweeded tennis court,
the empty garage, windows heavily shuttered.

Mrs. Vandergast took the children
and went back to her family.

And Vandergast moved to New Jersey,
where he works for an insurance company
whose emblem is the Rock of Gibraltar—
the rest of his life laid out
with the child-support and alimony payments.

As for the girl, she vanished.

Was it worth it? Ask Vandergast.
You'd have to be Vandergast, looking through his eyes
at the house across the street, in Orange, New Jersey.

Maybe on wet days umbrellas and raincoats
set his heart thudding.

         Maybe
he talks to his pillow and it whispers,
moving red hair.

In any case, he will soon be forty.

On a Disappearance of the Moon

And I, who used to lie with the moon,
am here in a peat-bog.

With a criminal, an adulterous girl,
and a witch tied down with branches . . .

the glaucous eyeballs gleaming
under the lids, some hairs still on the chin.

Port Jefferson

My whole life coming to this place,
and understanding it better
maybe for having been born
offshore, and at an early age
left to my own support . . .

I have come where sea and wind,
wave and leaf, are one sighing,
where the house strains at an anchor
and the salt-rose clings and clambers
on the humorous grave.

This is the place, Camerado,
that hides the seabird's nest.
Listening to the distant voices
in summer, a murmur of the sea,
I seem to remember everything.

A Friend of the Family

1

Once upon a time in California
the ignorant married the inane
and they lived happily ever after.

But nowadays in the villas
with swimming pools shaped like a kidney
technicians are beating their wives.
They're accusing each other of mental cruelty.

And the children of those parents
are longing for a rustic community.
They want to get back to the good old days.

Coming toward me . . . a slender
sad girl dressed like a sailor . . .
she says, "Do you have any change?"

One morning when the Mother Superior
was opening another can of furniture polish
Cyd ran for the bus
and came to San Francisco.
Now she drifts from pad to pad. "Hey mister,"
she says, "do you have any change?
I mean, for a hamburger. Really."

2

Let Yevtushenko celebrate the construction
of a hydroelectric dam.
For Russians a dam that works is a miracle.

Why should we celebrate it?
There are lights in the mountain states,
 sanatoriums, and the music of Beethoven.

Why should we celebrate the construction
of a better bowling alley?
Let Yevtushenko celebrate it.

A hundred, that's how ancient it is
with us, the rapture of material conquest,

democracy "draining a swamp,
turning the course of a river."

The dynamo howls
but the psyche is still, like an Indian.

And those who are still distending the empire
have vanished beyond our sight.
Far from the sense of hearing
and touch, they are merging
with Asia . . .

expanding the war on nature
and the old know-how to Asia.

Nowadays if we want that kind of excitement—
selling beads and whiskey to Indians,
setting up a feed store,
a market in shoes, tires, machine guns,
material ecstasy, money with hands and feet
stacked up like wooden Indians . . .

we must go out to Asia,
or rocketing outward in space.

3

What are they doing in Russia
these nights for entertainment?

In our desert where gas pumps shine
the women are changing their hair—
bubbles of gold and magenta . . .
and the young men yearning to be off
full speed . . . like Chichikov

in a troika-rocket, plying
the whip, while stars go flying
(Too bad for the off-beat horse!)

These nights when a space-rocket rises
and everyone sighs, "That's Progress!"
I say to myself, "That's Chichikov."
As it is right here on earth—
Osteopaths on Mars,
Actuaries at the Venus-Hilton . . .
Chichikov talking, Chichikov eating,
Chichikov making love.

"Hey Chichikov, where are you going?"

"I'm off to the moon," says Chichikov.

"What will you do when you get there?"

"How do I know?" says Chichikov.

4

Andrei, that fish you caught was my uncle.
He lived in Lutsk, not to be confused
with Lodz which is more famous.

When he was twenty he wrote to Chekhov,
and an answer came—"Come to us."
And there it was, signed "Chekhov."

I can see him getting on the train.
It was going to the great city
where Jews had been forbidden.

He went directly to Chekhov's house.
At the door he saw a crowd . . .
they told him that Chekhov had just died.

So he went back to his village.
Years passed . . . he danced at a wedding
and wept at a funeral.

Then, when Hitler sent for the Jews
he said, "And don't forget Isidor . . .
turn left at the pickle-factory."

Andrei, all my life I've been haunted
by Russia—a plain,
a cold wind from the *shtetl*.

I can hear the wheels of the train.
It is going to Radom,
it is going to Jerusalem.

In the night where candles shine
I have a luminous family . . .
people with their arms round each other
forever.

5

I can see myself getting off the train.
"Say, can you tell me how to get . . ."

To Chekhov's house perhaps?

That's what everyone wants, and yet
Chekhov was just a man . . . with ideas,
it's true. As I said to him once,
where on earth do you meet those people?

Vanya who is long-suffering
and Ivanov who is drunk.
And the man, I forget his name,
who thinks everything is forbidden . . .
that you have to have permission
to run, to shout . . .

And the people who say, "Tell us,
what is it you do exactly to justify your existence?"

These idiots rule the world,
Chekhov knew it, and yet
I think he was happy, on his street.
People live here . . . you'd be amazed.

The Foggy Lane

The houses seem to be floating
in the fog, like lights at sea.

Last summer I came here with a man
who spoke of the ancient Scottish poets—
how they would lie blindfolded,
with a stone placed on the belly,
and so compose their panegyrics . . .
while we, being comfortable,
find nothing to praise.

Then I came here with a radical
who said that everything is corrupt;
he wanted to live in a pure world.

And a man from an insurance company
who said that I needed "more protection."

Walking in the foggy lane
I try to keep my attention fixed
on the uneven, muddy surface . . .
the pools made by the rain,
and wheel ruts, and wet leaves,
and the rustling of small animals.

Sacred Objects

I am taking part in a great experiment—
whether writers can live peacefully in the suburbs
and not be bored to death.

As Whitman said, an American muse
installed amid the kitchen ware.
And we have wonderful household appliances . . .
now tell me about the poets.

Where are your children, Lucina?
Since Eliot died and Pound
has become . . . an authority,
chef d'école au lieu d'être tout de go,

I have been listening to the whispers
of U.S. Steel and Anaconda:
"In a little while it will stiffen . . .
blown into the road,

drifting with the foam of chemicals."

The light that shines through the *Leaves*
is clear: "to form individuals."

A swamp where the seabirds brood.
When the psyche is still and the soul does nothing,
a Sound, with shining tidal pools and channels.

And the kingdom is within you . . .

the hills and all the streams
running west to the Mississippi.
There the roads are lined with timothy
and the clouds are tangled with the haystacks.

Your loves are a line of birch trees.
When the wind flattens the grass, it
shines, and a butterfly
writes dark lines on the air.

There are your sacred objects,
the wings and gazing eyes
of the life you really have.

3

Where then shall we meet?

                    Where you left me.
At the drive-in restaurant . . .
the fields on either side covered with stubble,
an odor of gasoline and burning asphalt,
glare on tinted glass, chrome-plated hubcaps and bumpers.

I came out, wiping my hands
on my apron, to take your orders.
Thin hands, streaked with mustard,
give us a hot dog,
give us a Pepsi-Cola.

Listening to the monotonous grasshoppers
for years I have concentrated on the moment.

And at night when the passing headlights hurl
shadows flitting across the wall,
I sit in a window, combing my hair
day in day out.

Trasimeno

When Hannibal defeated the Roman army
he stopped at Trasimeno.

That day, and the next, he marched no further.
His tent lay in the moonlight,

his sword shone in the moonlight,
what thought kept him from moving, no one knows.

Stranger, when you go to Rome,
when you have placed your hand in the gargoyle's mouth,

and walked in the alleys . . .
when you have satisfied your hunger for stone,

at night you will return to the trees
and the ways of the barbarians,

hands, eyes, voices, ephemera,
shadows of the African horsemen.

The Peat-Bog Man

He was one of the consorts of the moon,
and went with the goddess in a cart.

Wherever he went there would be someone,
a few of the last of the old religion.

Here the moon passes behind a cloud.
Fifteen centuries pass,

then one of the bog-peat cutters
digs up the man—with the rope

that ends in a noose at the throat—
a head squashed like a pumpkin.

Yet, there is delicacy in the features
and a peaceful expression . . .

that in Spring the flower comes forth
with a music of pipes and dancing.

The Silent Piano

We have lived like civilized people.
O ruins, traditions!

And we have seen the barbarians,
breakers of sculpture and glass.

And now we talk of "the inner life,"
and I ask myself, where is it?

Not here, in these streets and houses,
so I think it must be found

in indolence, pure indolence,
an ocean of darkness,

in silence, an arm of the moon,
a hand that enters slowly.

*

I am reminded of a story
Camus tells, of a man in prison camp.

He had carved a piano keyboard
with a nail on a piece of wood.

And sat there playing the piano.
This music was made entirely of silence.

from
SEARCHING FOR THE OX

1976

Venus in the Tropics

1

One morning when I went over to Bournemouth
it was crowded with American sailors—
chubby faces like Jack Oakie
chewing gum and cracking wise.

Pushing each other into the pool,
bellyflopping from the diving boards,
piling on the raft to sink it,
hanging from the rings, then letting go.

Later, when I went into Kingston
to exchange some library books,
they were everywhere, buying souvenirs,
calabash gourds, and necklaces made of seeds.

On Saturday night at the Gaiety
they kept talking and making a noise.
When the management asked them to stop
they told it to get wise, to fly a kite, to scram.

2

We drove down to Harbour Street
with Mims ("She isn't your mother.
You ought to call her by some affectionate nickname—
why don't you call her Mims?")

There were two American cruisers,
the turrets and guns distinctly visible,
and some destroyers—I counted four.

The crews were coming ashore in launches.
As each group walked off the dock
we noticed a number of women
wearing high heels. They went up to the sailors
and engaged them in conversation.

"You've seen enough," said Mims.
"In fact, you may have seen too much."
She started the Buick, shifting into gear
swiftly with a gloved hand.

She always wore gloves and a broad hat.
To protect her complexion, she told us.
She was extremely sensitive.
All redheaded people were.

"She's a redhead, like Clara Bow,"
our father wrote in his letter.

"The Red Death," said my grandmother
twenty years later, on Eastern Parkway
in Brooklyn. We were talking about my father.
She thought he must have been ill—
not in his right mind—to marry a typist
and leave her practically everything.

How else to explain it, such an intelligent man?

3

The American warships left.
Then the *Empress of Britain*
came and stayed for a few days
during which the town was full of tourists.
Then, once more, the harbor was empty.

I sat by the pool at Bournemouth
reading *Typhoon.*
I had the pool all to myself,
the raft, the diving boards, and the rings.
There wasn't a living soul.

Not a voice—just rustling palm leaves
and the tops of the coconuts
moving around in circles.

In the afternoon a wind sprang up,
blowing from the sea to land,
covering the harbor with whitecaps.

It smelled of shells and seaweed,
and something else—perfume.

Dinner at the Sea-View Inn

1

Peter said, "I'd like some air."

"That's a good idea," said Marie's father.
"Why don't you young people go for a walk?"

Marie glanced at her mother.
Something passed between them. A warning.

2

When Peter and Marie walked through the dining room
everyone stared.

I just think so,
he reminded himself, and said,
"Fitzgerald says that nobody thinks about us
as much as we think they do."

"Who's he?" said Marie. "Another of your favorite authors?"

3

She wanted to know where he was taking her.

"I just had to get out of there.
Wouldn't it be great to hire a taxi
and just keep going?"

"Why?" said Marie.

"It's a wonderful night."

"I'd rather have my own car," said Marie.

4

"I'm getting cold," said Marie.
"How much further are we going?"

"All right," he said.

And they walked back.

"When I was a child," said Peter,
"I used to think that the waves were cavalry . . .
the way they come in, curling over."

She said, "Is that what you were in,
the calvary?" He laughed. "Calvary? For Christ's sake . . ."

5

"Did you have a good walk?" said Marie's father.

Marie said something to her mother.

Shortly after, Mr. Shulman ordered the car,
and they all drove back to New York.

They let Peter out in front of his building
on West Eighty-fourth Street, saying goodnight.
All but Marie . . . She still sat stiffly,
unsmiling. She had been offended.

6

Everything was just as he'd left it . . .
the convertible couch,
the reading lamp and chair,
and the stand with the typewriter.

He undressed and went to bed,
and turned out the light.

Lying in bed, hands clasped beneath his head,
listening . . .

to the stopping and starting of traffic
in the street five floors below.
And the opening of the elevator,
and the sound of feet going down the corridor.

The Springs at Gadara

I spent five years in publishing—
feet on the bottom desk drawer, the foetal position,
reading *Crossways, A Novel*
and *The Life of Elbert Hubbard.*

At day's end, depending on the weather,
I would walk—acrosstown and up,
sometimes uptown and across.
Looking in the windows exhibiting
golf, ice skates, ski equipment,
Sweetville Candy U. S. A.,
a tour of France or Italy.
At the movie marquee advertising
No Morals and *Midnight Frolics Adults Only.*

Autumn is best, the feeling of excitement
at twilight, the lights going on.
Beauty moves in the crowd up ahead
on the avenue. There she is again—
a flash of color vanishing
in the cool, illusory air.
Where is she going? Who lives where she lives?

Then I would be in the side streets
with Jesus signs and boarded windows.
Not because I am underpaid,
I told myself. I like these shabby streets
where everything is expected.

I would climb three flights to the apartment,
and flop. Then it was dark, with lights
going by, flashes on the ceiling.

So, without effort, time was passing.
I might have fought for Israel.
I might have been writing a novel
the size of Proust's. Two pages a day
for five years—you figure it!
There were times when I would try to write,
but soon tire, taking off my glasses
and covering my eyes. Like Swann.
This would set off a train of thought.

Finally I'd say to hell with it,
and decide to spend another evening with Gallagher.

He too was in publishing. We used to go to parties
and meet successful authors.
They didn't sit around discussing *le mot juste*—
they talked about their royalties,
and the latest rumors—what Paramount
had paid for the movie rights
to the new novel by Jones, Capote or Mailer.

Gallagher drank. One evening
when I arrived, his door was open.
He was lying on the floor, dead drunk.
He had left the phonograph on,
the turntable going around,
playing "My Funny Valentine" over and over.

When I look back at myself
it is like looking through a window
and seeing another person.
I see him trying to lift Gallagher
onto the sofa. Then giving it up.
He comes across to the window
and stands there, looking out.

Who knows, there may be another,
a third, who from where he stands
in the night can see us both.

*

One day I was leafing through a manuscript
taken at random from the slush pile.
It was titled *The Springs at Gadara.*

The epigraph explained: there once was a philosopher
named Jamblicus, who by magic raised
the spirits of Eros and Anteros
close by the springs at Gadara.

Anteros . . . I stared at the name.
Eros I knew, but Anteros . . .

Words are realities. They have the power
to make us feel and see.
I had a vision of an oasis
and some Arabs sitting on the ground.

And myself, in the midst of it,
chained to a horizontal beam.
I was pushing it around in a circle,
and a heavy millstone rolled
in a groove as the beam went around.

All the time I had spent in publishing,
sitting at a desk . . . actually, I had been laboring
under a spell. Anteros.
It was time for Eros to put in an appearance.

As I thought so, the chain fell off.
I started walking away.
Nothing sprang up behind me
and no one uttered a sound.

When I had gone some distance
I looked back. There was the oasis,
the palm trees, and the Arabs
in the same positions, sitting on the ground.

I could see the horizontal beam
and some other poor devil pushing it,
making the stone go around.

The Hour of Feeling

Love, now a universal birth,
From heart to heart is stealing,
From earth to man, from man to earth:
—It is the hour of feeling.

WORDSWORTH, *To My Sister*

A woman speaks:
"I hear you were in San Francisco.
What did they tell you about me?"

She begins to tremble. I can hear the sound
her elbow made, rapping on the wood.
It was something to see and to hear—
not like the words that pass for life,
things you read about in the papers.

People who read a deeper significance
into everything, every whisper . . .
who believe that a knife crossed with a fork
is a signal . . . by the sheer intensity
of their feeling leave an impression.

And with her, tangled in her hair,
came the atmosphere, four walls,
the avenues of the city
at twilight, the lights going on.

When I left I started to walk.
Once I stopped to look at a window
displaying ice skates and skis.
At another with Florsheim shoes . . .

Thanks to the emotion with which she spoke
I can see half of Manhattan,
the canyons and the avenues.

There are signs high in the air
above Times Square and the vicinity:
a sign for Schenley's Whiskey,
for Admiral Television,
and a sign saying Milltag, whatever that means.

I can see over to Brooklyn and Jersey,
and beyond there are meadows,
and mountains and plains.

The Mannequins

Whenever I passed Saks Fifth Avenue
I would stop at a certain window.
They didn't acknowledge my presence—they just stared.

He was sitting in his favorite chair,
smoking a pipe and reading a best seller.
She was standing in front of an easel.

She was finding it easy to paint
by filling in the numbered spaces
with colors. $5.98.

The artificial logs glowed in the fireplace.
Soon it would be Christmas. Santa would come down the chimney,
and they'd give each other presents.

She would give him skis and cuff links.
He would give her a watch with its works exposed,
and a fur coat, and perfume.

Though I knew it was "neurasthenic"
I couldn't help listening to the words
that they said without moving their lips.

The Middleaged Man

There is a middleaged man, Tim Flanagan,
whom everyone calls "Fireball."
Every night he does the rocket-match trick.
"Ten, nine, eight . . ." On zero
pfft! It flies through the air.

Walking to the subway with Flanagan . . .
He tells me that he lives out in Queens
on Avenue Street, the end of the line.
That he "makes his home" with his sister
who has recently lost her husband.

What is it to me?
Yet I can't help imagining what it would be like
to be Flanagan. Climbing the stairs
and letting himself in . . .
I can see him eating in the kitchen.

He stays up late watching television.
From time to time he comes to the window.
At this late hour the streets are deserted.
He looks up and down. He looks right at me,
then he steps back out of sight.

*

Sometimes I wake in the middle of the night
and I have a vision of Flanagan.
He is wearing an old pair of glasses
with a wire bent around the ear
and fastened to the frame with tape.

He is reading a novel by Morley Callaghan.
Whenever I wake he is still there . . .
with his glasses. I wish he would get them fixed.
I cannot sleep as long as there is wire
running from his eye to his ear.

Baruch

There is an old folk saying:
"He wishes to study the Torah
but he has a wife and family."
Baruch had a sincere love of learning
but he owned a dress-hat factory.

One night he was in his cart returning
to the village. Falling asleep . . .
All at once he uttered a cry
and snatched up the reins. He flew!
In the distance there was fire
and smoke. It was the factory,
the factory that he owned was burning.

All night it burned, and by daylight
Lev Baruch was a ruined man.
Some said that it was gypsies,
that sparks from their fire set it burning.
Others said, the workers.

But Lev never murmured. To the contrary,
he said, "It is written,
'by night in a pillar of fire.'"
He said, "Every day of my life
I had looked for a sign in that direction.
Now that I have been relieved of my property
I shall give myself to the Word."

And he did from that day on,
reading Rashi and Maimonides.
He was half way over the *Four Mountains*
when one day, in the midst of his studying,

Lev Baruch fell sick and died.
For in Israel it is also written,
"Prophecy is too great a thing for Baruch."

II

They were lovers of reading in the family.
For instance, Cousin Deborah
who, they said, had read everything . . .
The question was, which would she marry,
Tolstoy or Lermontov or Pushkin?

But her family married her off
to a man from Kiev, a timber merchant
who came from Kiev with a team of horses.
On her wedding day she wept,
and at night when they locked her in
she kicked and beat on the door.
She screamed. So much for the wedding!
As soon as it was daylight, Brodsky—
that was his name—drove back to Kiev
like a man pursued, with his horses.

III

We have been devoted to words.
Even here in this rich country
Scripture enters and sits down
and lives with us like a relative.
Taking the best chair in the house . . .

His eyes go everywhere, not missing anything.
Wherever his looks go, something ages
and suddenly tears or falls.
Here, a worn place in the carpet,
there, a crack in the wall.

The love of literature goes with us.

On a train approaching midnight
everyone else has climbed into his sarcophagus
except four men playing cards.
There is nothing better than poker—
not for the stakes but the companionship,
trying to outsmart one another.
Taking just one card . . .

I am sitting next to the window,
looking at the lights on the prairie
clicking by. From time to time
two or three will come together
then go wandering off again.

Then I see a face, pale and unearthly,
that is flitting along with the train,
passing over the fields and rooftops,
and I hear a voice out of the past:
"He wishes to study the Torah."

Searching for the Ox

1

I have a friend who works in a mental hospital.
Sometimes he talks of his patients.
There is one, a schizophrenic:
she was born during the Korean War
and raised on an Air Force base.
Then the family moved to La Jolla.
At fourteen she started taking speed
because everyone else was taking it.

Father, I too have my cases:
hands, eyes, voices, ephemera.
They want me to see how they live.
They single me out in a crowd, at a distance,
the one face that will listen
to any incoherent, aimless story.
Then for years they hang around—
"Hey listen!"—tugging at a nerve.
 Like the spirits Buddhists call
"hungry ghosts." And when they sense an opening,
rush in. So they are born
and live. So they continue.

There is something in disorder that calls to me.
Out there beyond the harbor
where, every night, the lighthouse
probes the sea with its feathery beam,
something is rising to the surface.
It lies in the darkness breathing,
it floats on the waves regarding
this luminous world,
lights that are shining round the shoreline.
It snorts and splashes,

then rolls its blackness like a tube
back to the bottom.

At dusk when the lamps go on
I have stayed outside and watched
the shadow-life of the interior,
feeling myself apart from it.
A feeling of—as though I were made of glass.
Or the balloon I once saw in Florida
in a swimming pool, with a string
trailing in loops on the surface.
Suddenly the balloon went swiveling
on the water, trying to lift.
Then drifted steadily, being driven
from one side of the pool to the other.

2

There is a light in a window opposite.

All over the world . . . in China
and Africa, they are turning the pages.
All that is necessary is to submit
to engineering, law—one of the disciplines
that, when you submit, drive you forward.

There have been great strides in space.

On a flight leaving Kennedy
I have heard the engineers from IBM
speaking slide rule and doing their calculations.
I saw the first men leave for the moon:
how the rocket clawed at the ground
at first, reluctant to lift;
how it rose, and climbed, and curved,
punching a round, black hole in a cloud.

Before I got back to Orlando
it had been twice round the world.

And still, I must confess,
I fear those *messieurs,* like a peasant
listening to the priests talk Latin.
They will send me off to Heaven
when all I want is to live in the world.

3

The search for the ox continues.
I read in the *Times,* there are young men in Osaka
called Moles. They live underground
in the underground shopping center.
They cut a joint off their little finger,
and they say, "All Al Capone."

I have a friend who has left America—
he finds it more pleasant living in Italy.

O ruins, traditions!
Past a field full of stones,
the ruins of vine-wreathed brickwork,
the road in a soundless march continues
forever into the past.

I have sat in the field full of stones—
stones of an archway, stones
of the columns of the temple,
stones carved S.P.Q.R.,
stones that have been shaped
as women are . . .
Limbs of the gods that have fallen,
too cumbersome to be borne.

By the lake at Trasimeno . . .
If Hannibal had not paused at Trasimeno
the history of the world would have been different.
How so? There would still be a sound
of lapping water, and leaves,

4

"As you have wasted your life here in this corner
you have ruined it all over the world."
This was written by Cavafy who lived in Alexandria.
Alexandria with blue awnings
that flap in the wind,
sea walls gleaming with reflections.
A steam winch raffles,
an anchor clanks,
smoke drifts over the rooftops,
and at night the lighted streets go sailing.

At night the gods come down—
The earth then seems so pleasant.
They pass through the murmuring crowd.
They are seen in the cafes and restaurants,
They prefer the voice of a child
or the face of a girl to their fame
in their high, cold palaces on Olympus.

In the evening the wind blows from the sea.
The wind rises and winds like a serpent
filling the diaphanous curtains
where the women sit: Mousmé,
Hélène, and the English girl.
When you pass, their lips make a sound,
twittering, like the swallows
in Cyprus that built their nests
in the temple, above the door.

Each one has a sweetheart far away.
They are making their trousseaux;
they don't make love, they knit.

In the bar down the street
a door keeps opening and closing.
Then a pair of heels go hurrying.
In the streets that lead down to the harbor
all night long there are footsteps
and opening doors. It is Eros
Peridromos, who never sleeps till dawn.

5

Following in the Way
that "regards sensory experience as relatively unimportant,"
and that aims to teach the follower
"to renounce what one is attached to"—
in spite of this dubious gift
that would end by negating poetry altogether,
in the practice of meditating
on the breath I find my awareness
of the world—the cry of a bird,
susurrus of tires, the wheezing
of the man in the chair next to me—
has increased. That every sound
falls like a pebble into a well,
sending out ripples that seem to be continuing
through the universe. Sound has a tail
that whips around the corner;
I try not to follow. In any case,
I find I am far more aware
of the present, sensory life.

I seem to understand what the artist
was driving at; every leaf stands clear

and separate. The twig seems to quiver
with intellect. Searching for the ox
I come upon a single hoofprint.
I find the ox, and tame it,
and lead it home. In the next scene
the moon has risen, a cool light.
Both the ox and herdsman vanished.

There is only earth:
in winter laden with snow,
in summer covered with leaves.

The Street

Here comes the subway grating fisher
letting down his line through the sidewalk.

Yesterday there was the running man
who sobbed and wept as he ran.

Today there is the subway grating fisher.
Standing as if in thought . . .

He fishes a while. Then winds up the line
and continues to walk, looking down.

Big Dream, Little Dream

The Elgonyi say, there are big dreams and little dreams.
The little dream is just personal. . . .
sitting in a plane that is flying
too close to the ground. There are wires . . .
on either side there's a wall.

The big dream feels significant.
The big dream is the kind the president has.
He wakes and tells it to the secretary,
together they tell it to the cabinet,
and before you know there is war.

Before the Poetry Reading

Composition for Voices, Dutch Banjo, Sick Flute, and a Hair Drum

1

This is the poetry reading.
This is the man who is going to give the poetry reading.
He is standing in a street in which the rain is falling
With his suitcase open on the roof of a car for some reason,
And the rain falling into the suitcase,
While the people standing nearby say,
"If you had come on a Monday,
Or a Tuesday, or a Thursday,
If you had come on a Wednesday,
Or on any day but this,
You would have had an audience,
For we here at Quinippiac (Western or Wretched State U.)
Have wonderful audiences for poetry readings."
By this time he has closed the suitcase
And put it on the back seat, which is empty,
But on the front seat sit Saul Bellow,
James Baldwin, and Uncle Rudy and Fanya.
They are upright, not turning their heads, their fedoras straight on,
For they know where they are going,
And you should know, so they do not deign to answer
When you say, "Where in Hell is this car going?"
Whereupon, with a leap, slamming the door shut,
Taking your suitcase with it, and your Only Available Manuscript,
And leaving you standing there,
The car leaps into the future,
Still raining, in which its taillight disappears.
And a man who is still looking on
With his coat collar turned up, says.
"If you had come on a Friday,
A Saturday or a Sunday.

Or if you had come on a Wednesday
Or a Tuesday, there would have been an audience.
For we here at Madagascar
And the University of Lost Causes
Have wonderful audiences for poetry readings."

2

This is the man who is going to introduce you.
He says, "Could you tell me the names
Of the books you have written.
And is there anything you would like me to say?"

3

This is the lady who is giving a party for you
After the poetry reading.
She says, "I hope you don't mind, but
I have carefully avoided inviting
Any beautiful, attractive, farouche young women,
But the Vicar of Dunstable is coming,
Who is over here this year on an exchange program,
And the Calvinist Spiritual Chorus Society,
And all the members of the Poetry Writing Workshop."

4

This is the man who has an announcement to make.
He says, "I have a few announcements.
First, before the poetry reading starts,
If you leave the building and walk rapidly
Ten miles in the opposite direction,
A concert of music and poetry is being given
By Wolfgang Amadeus Mozart and William Shakespeare.

Also, during the intermission
There is time for you to catch the rising
Of the Latter Day Saints at the Day of Judgement.
Directly after the reading,
If you turn left, past the Community Building,
And walk for seventeen miles,
There is tea and little pieces of eraser
Being served in the Gymnasium.
Last week we had a reading by Dante,
And the week before by Sophocles;
A week from tonight, Saint Francis of Assisi will appear in person—
But tonight I am happy to introduce
Mister Willoughby, who will make the introduction
Of our guest, Mr. . . ."

from
CAVIAR AT THE FUNERAL

1980

Working Late

A light is on in my father's study.
"Still up?" he says, and we are silent,
looking at the harbor lights,
listening to the surf
and the creak of coconut boughs.

He is working late on cases.
No impassioned speech! He argues from evidence,
actually pacing out and measuring,
while the fans revolving on the ceiling
winnow the true from the false.

Once he passed a brass curtain rod
through a head made out of plaster
and showed the jury the angle of fire—
where the murderer must have stood.
For years, all through my childhood,
if I opened a closet . . . bang!
There would be the dead man's head
with a black hole in the forehead.

All the arguing in the world
will not stay the moon.
She has come all the way from Russia
to gaze for a while in a mango tree
and light the wall of a veranda,
before resuming her interrupted journey
beyond the harbor and the lighthouse
at Port Royal, turning away
from land to the open sea.

Yet, nothing in nature changes, from that day to this,
she is still the mother of us all.

I can see the drifting offshore lights,
black posts where the pelicans brood.

And the light that used to shine
at night in my father's study
now shines as late in mine.

Sway

Swing and sway with Sammy Kaye.

Everyone at Lake Kearney had a nickname:
there was a Bumstead, a Tonto, a Tex,
and, from the slogan of a popular orchestra,
two sisters, Swing and Sway.

Swing jitterbugged, hopping around
on the dance floor, working up a sweat.
Sway was beautiful. My heart went out to her
when she lifted her heavy rack of dishes
and passed through the swinging door.

She was engaged, to an enlisted man
who was stationed at Fort Dix.
He came once or twice on weekends
to see her. I tried talking to him,
but he didn't answer . . . out of stupidity
or dislike, I could not tell which.
In real life he was a furniture salesman.
This was the hero on whom she had chosen
to bestow her affections.

I told her of my ambition:
to write novels conveying the excitement
of life . . . the main building lit up
like a liner on Saturday night;
the sound of the band . . . clarinet,
saxophone, snare drum, piano.
He who would know your heart (America)
must seek it in your songs.

And the contents of your purse . . .
among Kleenex, aspirin,
chewing gum wrappers, combs, et cetera.

"Don't stop," she said, "I'm listening.
Here it is!" flourishing her lighter.

*

In the afternoon when the dishes were washed
and tables wiped, we rowed out on the lake.
I read aloud . . . the *Duino Elegies,*
while she reclined, one shapely knee up,
trailing a hand in the water.

She had chestnut-colored hair.
Her eyes were changing like the surface
with ripples and the shadows of clouds.

"Beauty," I read to her, "is nothing
but beginning of Terror we're still just able to bear."

*

She came from Jersey, the industrial wasteland
behind which Manhattan suddenly rises.
I could visualize the street where she lived,
and see her muffled against the cold,
in galoshes, trudging to school.
Running about in tennis shoes
all through the summer . . .
I could hear the porch swing squeak
and see into the parlor.
It was divided by a curtain or screen. . . .

"That's it," she said, "all but the screen.
There isn't any."

When she or her sister had a boyfriend
their mother used to stay in the parlor,
pretending to sew, and keeping an eye on them
like Fate.

At night she would lie awake
looking at the sky, spangled over.
Her thoughts were as deep and wide as the sky.
As time went by she had a feeling
of missing out . . . that everything
was happening somewhere else.

Some of the kids she grew up with
went crazy . . . like a car turning over and over.
One of her friends had been beaten
by the police. Some vital fluid
seemed to have gone out of him.
His arms and legs shook. Busted springs.

*

She said, "When you're a famous novelist
will you write about me?"

I promised . . . and tried to keep my promise.

Recently, looking for a toolbox,
I came upon some typewritten pages,
all about her. There she is
in a canoe . . . a gust of wind
rustling the leaves along the shore.
Playing tennis, running up and down the baseline.
Down by the boathouse, listening to the orchestra
playing "Sleepy Lagoon."

Then the trouble begins. I can never think of anything
to make the characters do.

We are still sitting in the moonlight
while she finishes her cigarette.
Two people go by, talking in low voices.
A car door slams. Driving off . . .

"I suppose we ought to go,"
I say.

     And she says, "Not yet."

American Classic

It's a classic American scene—
a car stopped off the road
and a man trying to repair it.

The woman who stays in the car
in the classic American scene
stares back at the freeway traffic.

They look surprised, and ashamed
to be so helpless . . .
let down in the middle of the road!

To think that their car would do this!
They look like mountain people
whose son has gone against the law.

But every night they set out food
and the robber goes skulking back to the trees.
That's how it is with the car . . .

it's theirs, they're stuck with it.
Now they know what it's like to sit
and see the world go whizzing by.

In the fume of carbon monoxide and dust
they are not such good Americans
as they thought they were.

The feeling of being left out
through no fault of your own is common.
That's why I say, an American classic.

The Beaded Pear

Kennst du das Land, wo die Zitronen blühn?
GOETHE, *MIGNON*

1
Shopping

Dad in Bermuda shorts, Mom her hair in curlers,
Jimmy, sixteen, and Darlene who is twelve,
are walking through the Smith Haven Mall.

Jimmy needs a new pair of shoes.
In the Mall by actual count
there are twenty-two stores selling shoes:
Wise Shoes, Regal Shoes,
National Shoes, Naturalizer Shoes,
Stride Rite, Selby, Hanover . . .

Dad has to buy a new lock for the garage,
Mom and Darlene want to look at clothes.
They agree to meet again in an hour
at the fountain.

The Mall is laid out like a cathedral
with two arcades that cross—
Macy's at one end of the main arcade,
Abraham and Straus at the other.
At the junction of transept and nave
there is a circular, sunken area
with stairs where people sit,
mostly teenagers, smoking
and making dates to meet later.
This is what is meant by "at the fountain."

2
"Why Don't You Get Transferred, Dad?"

One of Jimmy's friends comes by in his car,
and Jimmy goes out. "Be careful,"
Mom says. He has to learn to drive,
but it makes her nervous thinking about it.

Darlene goes over to see Marion
whose father is being transferred
to a new branch of the company
in Houston. "Why don't you get transferred, Dad?"

"I'd like to," he replies.
"I'd also like a million dollars."

This is a constant topic in the family:
where else you would like to live.
Darlene likes California—
"It has beautiful scenery
and you get to meet all the stars."
Mom prefers Arizona, because of a picture
she saw once, in *Good Housekeeping.*
Jimmy doesn't care,
and Dad likes it here. "You can find anything
you want right where you are."
He reminds them of *The Wizard of Oz,*
about happiness, how it is found
right in your own backyard.

Dad's right, Mom always says.
The Wizard of Oz is a tradition
in the family. They see it every year.

3
The Beaded Pear

The children are home at six,
and they sit down to eat. Mom insists
on their eating together at least once
every week. It keeps the family together.

After helping with the dishes
the children go out again,
and Mom and Dad settle down to watch
"Hollywood Star Time," with Bobby Darin,
Buddy Rich, Laura Nyro,
Judy Collins, and Stevie Wonder

When this is over he looks in *TV Guide,*
trying to decide
whether to watch "Salty O'Rourke (1945).
A gambler who is readying his horse
for an important race
falls in love with a pretty teacher,"
or, "Delightful family fare,
excellent melodrama of the Mafia."

She has seen enough television
for one night. She gets out the beaded pear
she bought today in the Mall.

A "Special $1.88 Do-it-yourself Beaded Pear.
No gluing or sewing required.
Beautiful beaded fruit is easily assembled
using enclosed pins, beads, and decorative material."

She says, "It's not going to be so easy."

"No," he says, "it never is."

She speaks again. "There is a complete series.
Apple, Pear, Banana, Lemon, Orange,
Grapes, Strawberry, Plum, and Lime."

The Ice Cube Maker

Once the ice was in a tray.
You would hold it under a faucet
till the cubes came unstuck, in a block.
Then you had to run more water over it
until, finally, the cubes came loose.

Later on, there was a handle you lifted,
breaking out the ice cubes.
But still it was a nuisance—
in order to get at one ice cube
you had to melt the whole tray.

Then they invented the ice cube maker
which makes cubes individually,
letting them fall in a container
until it is full, when it stops.
You can just reach in and take ice cubes.

*

When her husband came home he saw that she was drunk.
He changed into an old shirt and slacks.
He stared at the screen door in the kitchen . . .
the screen had to be replaced.
He wondered what he was doing. Why fix it?

The Old Graveyard at Hauppauge

In Adam's fall we sinned all,
and fell out of Paradise
into mankind—this body of salt
and gathering of the waters,
birth, work, and wedding garment.

But now we are at rest . . .
Aletta and Phebe Almira,
and Augusta Brunce, and the MacCrones . . .
lying in the earth, looking up
at the clouds and drifting trees.

Why Do You Write About Russia?

When I was a child
my mother told stories about the country
she came from. Wolves were howling,
snow fell, the drunken Cossack
shouted in the snow.

Rats prowled the floor of the cellar
where the children slept.
Once, after an illness, she was sent
to Odessa, on the sea. There were battleships
painted white, and ladies and gentlemen
walking the esplanade . . . white naval uniforms
and parasols.

These stories were told
against a background of tropical night . . .
a sea breeze stirring the flowers
that open at dusk, smelling like perfume.
The voice that spoke of freezing cold
itself was warm and infinitely comforting.

So it is with poetry: whatever numbing horrors
it may speak of, the voice itself
tells of love and infinite wonder.

Later, when I came to New York,
I used to go to my grandmother's
in Brooklyn. The names of stations
return in their order like a charm:
Franklin, Nostrand, Kingston.
And members of the family gather:
the three sisters, the one brother,
one of the cousins from Washington,

and myself . . . a "student at Columbia."
But what am I really?

For when my grandmother says "Eat!
People who work with their heads have to eat more.". . .
Work? Does it deserve a name
so full of seriousness and high purpose?

Gazing across Amsterdam Avenue
at the windows opposite, letting my mind
wander where it will, from the page
to Malaya, or some street in Paris . . .
Drifting smoke. The end will be as fatal
as an opium-eater's dream.

*

The view has changed—to evergreens
a hedge, and my neighbor's roof.
This too is like a dream, the way we live
with our cars and power mowers . . .
a life that shuns emotion
and the violence that goes with it,
the object being to live quietly
and bring up children to be happy.

Yes, but what are you going to tell them
of what lies ahead?
That the better life seems
the more it goes sour? The child no longer
a child, his happiness all of a sudden
behind him. And he in turn
expected to bring up his children
to be happy . . .

What then do I want?

A life in which there are depths
beyond happiness. As one of my friends,
Grigoryev, says, "Two things
constantly cry out in creation,
the sea and man's soul."

Reaching from where we are
to where we came from . . . *Thalassa!*
a view of the sea.

*

I sit listening to the rasp
of a power saw, the puttering of a motorboat.
The whole meaningless life around me
affirming a positive attitude . . .

When a hat appears, a black felt hat,
gliding along the hedge . . .
then a long, black overcoat
that falls beneath the knee.

He produces a big, purple handkerchief,
brushes off a chair, and sits.

"It's hot," he says, "but I like to walk,
that way you get to see the world.
And so, what are you reading now?"

Chekhov, I tell him.

"Of course. But have you read Leskov?
There are sentences that will stay in your mind
a whole lifetime.
For instance, in the 'Lady Macbeth,'
when the woman says to her lover,
'You couldn't be nearly as desirous

as you say you are, for I heard you singing' . . .
he answers, 'What about gnats?
They sing all their lives, but it's not for joy.' "

So my imaginary friend tells stories
of the same far place the soul comes from.

When I think about Russia
it's not that area of the earth's surface
with Leningrad to the West and Siberia
to the East—I don't know anything
about the continental mass.

It's a sound, such as you hear
in a sea breaking along a shore.

My people came from Russia,
bringing with them nothing
but that sound.

Typhus

"The whole earth was covered with snow,
and the Snow Queen's sleigh came gliding.
I heard the bells behind me,
and ran, and ran, till I was out of breath."

During the typhus epidemic
she almost died, and would have
but for the woman who lived next door
who cooked for her and watched by the bed.

When she came back to life
and saw herself in a mirror
they had cut off all her hair.
Also, they had burned her clothing,
and her doll, the only one she ever had,
made out of rags and a stick.

Afterwards, they sent her away
to Odessa, to stay with relatives.
The day she was leaving for home
she bought some plums, as a gift
to take back to the family.
They had never seen such plums!
They were in a window, in a basket.
To buy them she spent her last few kopecks.

The journey took three days by train.
It was hot, and the plums were beginning to spoil.
So she ate them . . .
until, finally, all were gone.
The people on the train were astonished.
A child who would eat a plum
and cry . . . then eat another!

*

Her sister, Lisa, died of typhus.
The corpse was laid on the floor.

They carried it to the cemetery
in a box, and brought back the box.
"We were poor—a box was worth something."

The Art of Storytelling

Once upon a time there was a *shocket*,
that is, a kosher butcher,
who went for a walk.

He was standing by the harbor
admiring the ships, all painted white,
when up came three sailors, led by an officer.
"Filth," they said, "who gave you permission?"
and they seized and carried him off.

So he was taken into the navy.
It wasn't a bad life—nothing is.
He learned how to climb and sew,
and to shout "Glad to be of service, Your Excellency!"
He sailed all round the world,
was twice shipwrecked, and had other adventures.
Finally, he made his way back to the village . . .
whereupon he put on his apron, and picked up his knife,
and continued to be a shocket.

At this point, the person telling the story
would say, "This shocket-sailor
was one of our relatives, a distant cousin."

It was always so, they knew they could depend on it.
Even if the story made no sense,
the one in the story would be a relative—
a definite connection with the family.

The Pawnshop

The first time I saw a pawnshop
I thought, Sheer insanity.
A revolver lying next to a camera,
violins hanging in the air like hams . . .

But in fact there was a reason for everything.

So it is with all these lives:
one is stained from painting with oils;
another has a way of arguing
with a finger along his nose, the Misnagid tradition;
a third sits at a desk made of mahogany.

They are all cunningly displayed
to appeal to someone. Each has its place in the universe.

Caviar at the Funeral

This was the village where the deacon ate all the caviar at the funeral.
CHEKHOV, *IN THE RAVINE*

On the way back from the cemetery
they discussed the funeral arrangements
and the sermon, "such a comfort to the family."

They crowded into the parlor.
It was hot, and voices were beginning to rise.
The deacon found himself beside a plate
heaped with caviar. He helped himself
to a spoonful. Then another.

Suddenly he became aware
that everyone's eyes were upon him,
ruin staring him in the face.
He turned pale. Then tried to carry it off—
one may as well be hanged for a sheep
as a lamb, et cetera.

Meeting their eyes with a stern expression
he took another spoonful, and another.
He finished the plate.

Next morning he was seen at the station
buying a ticket for Kurovskoye,
a village much like ours, only smaller.

Chocolates

Once some people were visiting Chekhov.
While they made remarks about his genius
the Master fidgeted. Finally
he said, "Do you like chocolates?"

They were astonished, and silent.
He repeated the question,
whereupon one lady plucked up her courage
and murmured shyly, "Yes."

"Tell me," he said, leaning forward,
light glinting from his spectacles,
"what kind? The light, sweet chocolate
or the dark, bitter kind?"

The conversation became general
They spoke of cherry centers,
of almonds and Brazil nuts.
Losing their inhibitions
they interrupted one another.
For people may not know what they think
about politics in the Balkans,
or the vexed question of men and women,

but everyone has a definite opinion
about the flavor of shredded coconut.
Finally someone spoke of chocolates filled with liqueur,
and everyone, even the author of *Uncle Vanya*,
was at a loss for words.

As they were leaving he stood by the door
and took their hands.

In the coach returning to Petersburg
they agreed that it had been a most
unusual conversation.

Armidale

Il faut voyager loin en aimant sa maison.
APOLLINAIRE

1
As a Man Walks

It's a strange country,
strange for me to have come to.
Cattle standing in a field,
sheep that are motionless
as stones,
the sun sinking in a pile of clouds,
and the eternal flies
getting in your ears and eyes . . .

I suppose you become accustomed.
Mrs. Scully was in her kitchen
entertaining two friends
when one said, "Isn't that a snake?"
and pointed. Sure enough
one was sliding around the divider.
She reached for something, the rolling pin,
and stunned it. Then finished it off
with a hammer.

The green-hide and stringy-bark Australian . . .
my candidate for survival
in the event of fire, flood,
or nuclear explosion.

As a man walks he creates the road he walks on.
All of my life in America
I must have been reeling out of myself
this red dirt, gravel road.

Three boys seated on motorcycles

conferring . . .

        A little further on,
a beaten-up Holden parked off the road
with two men inside passing the bottle.
Dark-skinned . . . maybe aboriginal.

I might have been content to live
in Belle Terre, among houses and lawns,
but inside me are gum trees,
and magpies, cackling and whistling,
and a bush-roaming kangaroo.

2
A Bush Band

A guitar and drum,
a pole with bottlecaps nailed to it . . .

Struck with a piece of wood
it gives off a silvery, joyful sound.

The woman playing the guitar
is sinewy, like the men in the ballad.

Driving their cattle overland
from Broome to Glen Garrick . . .

Cows low, wagon wheels turn,
red dust hangs in the air.

Some give their lives to cattle
and some to the words of a song,

arriving together at Glen Garrick
and at the end of the song.

Out of Season

Once I stayed at the Grand Hotel
at Beaulieu, on the Mediterranean.
This was in May. A wind blew steadily
from sea to land, banging the shutters.
Now and then a tile would go sailing.

At lunch and dinner we ate fish soup
with big, heavy spoons.
Then there would be fish, then the main course.

At the next table sat an old woman
and her companion, Miss O'Shaughnessy
who was always writing letters
on the desk in the lounge provided for that purpose—
along with copies of *Punch* and *The Tatler*
and an old wind-up Victrola.

There was a businessman from Sweden
and his secretary. She had a stunning figure
on the rocks down by the sea.
She told me, "My name is Helga.
From Vasteras" . . . brushing her hair,
leaning to the right, then to the left.

Also, an Englishman who looked ill
and went for walks by himself.

                    *

I remember a hotel in Kingston
where our mother used to stay
when she came on one of her visits
from America. It was called

the Manor House. There was a long veranda
outside our rooms, and peacocks on the lawn.

We played badminton and golf,
and went swimming at Myrtle Bank.
I did jigsaw puzzles, and water colors,
and read the books she had brought.

In the lounge there were newspapers
from America . . . "Gas House Gang Conquer Giants."
What I liked were the cartoons,
"The Katzenjammer Kids" and "Bringing Up Father."

᛫᛫᛫

Getting back to Beaulieu . . .
this could have been one of the places
where the Fitzgeralds used to stay—
the bedroom thirty feet across,
a ceiling twelve feet high.
The bathroom, also, was enormous.

A voice would say . . . "Avalon,"
followed by the sound of an orchestra,
and . . . shuffling. This would continue
all night, till two or three,
when the last pair of feet went away.

I was preparing to shave
when an arm came out of the wall.
It was holding a tennis racket.
It waved it twice, moved sideways,
flew up, and vanished through the ceiling.

*

Of course not. Yet, it's weird
how I remember the banging shutters
and the walk to the village
past cork trees and slopes lined with vines.

Narrow, cobbled streets going down to the sea . . .
There would be boats drawn up, and nets
that a fisherman was always mending.

I sat at a table overlooking the Mediterranean.
At the next table sat the Englishman
who looked unwell. I nodded.

He paid for his drink abruptly
and strode away. Terrified
that I might want his company.

*

At times like this, when I am away from home
or removed in some other way,
it is as though there were another self
that is waiting to find me alone.

Whereupon he steps forward:
"Here we are again, you and me . . .
and sounds . . . the chirping of birds
and whispering of leaves,
the sound of tires passing on the road."

Yes, and images . . . Miss O'Shaughnessy
shouting "Fish soup!" in the old woman's ear.
The businessman from Vasteras
and his girl . . . lying on her side,
the curve of her body
from head to slender feet.

The Englishman walking ahead of me . . .
He has a stick; as he walks
he slashes with it at the reeds
that are growing beside the road.

These things make an unforgettable impression,
as though there were a reason for being here,
in one place rather than another.

The Mexican Woman

All he needed was fifty cents
to get to a job in Union City.

You wouldn't believe it, he
was in Mexico with Black Jack Pershing.

He lived with a Mexican woman.
Then he followed her, and was wise.

"Baby," he said, "you're a two-timer,
I'm wise to you and the lieutenant."

                    *

I gave him the fifty cents,
but the old man's tale still haunts me.

I know what it's like to serve
in Mexico with Black Jack Pershing.

And to walk in the dust and heat . . .
for I can see her hurrying

to the clay wall where they meet,
and I shall be wise to her and the lieutenant.

Back in the States

It was cold, and all they gave him to wear
was a shirt. And he had malaria.

There was continual singing of hymns—
"Nearer My God to Thee" was a favorite.
And a sound like running water . . .
it took him a while to figure it.

Weeping, coming from the cells
of the men who had been condemned.

Now here he was, back in the States,
idly picking up a magazine,
glancing through the table of contents.

Already becoming like the rest of us.

from
THE BEST HOUR OF THE NIGHT

1983

Physical Universe

He woke at five and, unable
to go back to sleep,
went downstairs.

A book was lying on the table
where his son had done his homework.
He took it into the kitchen, made coffee,
poured himself a cup,
and settled down to read.

"There was a local eddy in the swirling gas
of the primordial galaxy,
and a cloud was formed, the protosun,
as wide as the present solar system.

"This contracted. Some of the gas
formed a diffuse, spherical nebula,
a thin disk, that cooled and flattened.
Pulled one way by its own gravity,
the other way by the sun,
it broke, forming smaller clouds,
the protoplanets. Earth
was 2,000 times as wide as it is now.

The earth was without form and void,
and darkness was upon the face of the deep.

                    *

"Then the sun began to shine,
dispelling the gases and vapors,
shrinking the planets, melting earth,
separating iron and silicate

to form the core and mantle.
Continents appeared . . ."

history, civilization,
the discovery of America
and the settling of Green Harbor,
bringing us to Tuesday, the seventh of July.

Tuesday, the day they pick up the garbage!
He leapt into action,
took the garbage bag out of its container,
tied it with a twist of wire,
and carried it out to the toolshed,
taking care not to let the screen door slam,
and put it in the large garbage can
that was three-quarters full.
He kept it in the toolshed so the raccoons
couldn't get at it.

He carried the can out to the road,
then went back into the house
and walked around, picking up newspapers
and fliers for: "Thompson Seedless Grapes,
California's Finest Sweet Eating";

"Scott Bathroom Tissue";

"Legislative Report from Senator Ken LaValle."

He put all this paper in a box,
and emptied the waste baskets in the two
downstairs bathrooms,
and the basket in the study.

He carried the box out to the road,
taking care not to let the screen door slam,
and placed the box next to the garbage.

Now let the garbage men come!

        *

He went back upstairs.
Mary said, "Did you put out the garbage?"
But her eyes were closed.
She was sleeping, yet could speak in her sleep,
ask a question, even answer one.

"Yes," he said, and climbed into bed.
She turned around to face him,
with her eyes still closed.

He thought, Perhaps she's an oracle,
speaking from the Collective Unconscious.
He said to her, "Do you agree with Darwin
that people and monkeys have a common ancestor?
Or should we stick to the Bible?"

She said, "Did you take out the garbage?"

"Yes," he said, for the second time.
Then thought about it. Her answer
had something in it of the sublime.
Like a *koan* . . . the kind of irrelevance
a Zen master says to the disciple
who is asking riddles of the universe.

He put his arm around her,
and she continued to breathe evenly
from the depths of sleep.

How to Live on Long Island

Lilco, $75.17;
Mastercard, $157.89;
Sunmark Industries, $94.03 . . .

Jim is paying his bills.
He writes out a check
and edges it into the envelope
provided by the company.
They always make them too small.

The print in the little box
in the top right corner informs him:
"The Post Office will not deliver
mail without proper postage."
They seem to know that the public
is composed of thieves and half-wits.

He seals the last envelope,
licks a stamp, sticks it on,
and with a feeling of virtue,
a necessary task accomplished,
takes the checks out to the mailbox.

It's a cool, clear night in Fall,
lights flickering through the leaves.
He thinks, All these families
with their situation comedies:
husbands writing checks,
wives studying fund-raising,
children locked in their rooms
listening to the music that appeals to them,
remind me of . . . fireflies
that shine for a night and die.

Of all these similar houses
what shall be left? Not even stones.
One could almost understand the pharaohs
with their pyramids and obelisks.

Every month when he pays his bills
Jim Bandy becomes a philosopher.
The rest of the time he's OK.

Jim has a hobby: fishing.
Last year he flew to Alaska.
Cold the salmon stream,
dark the Douglas firs,
and the pure stars are cold.

A bear came out of the forest.
Jim had two salmon . . . he threw one
but the bear kept coming.
He threw the other . . . it stopped.

The fish that are most memorable
he mounts, with a brass plate
giving the name and place and date:
Chinook Salmon, Red Salmon,
Brown Trout, Grouper,
Barracuda, Hammerhead Shark.

They do a lot of drinking in Alaska.
He saw thirty or forty lying drunk
in the street. And on the plane . . .

They cannot stand living in Alaska,
and he cannot stand Long Island
without flying to Alaska.

Quiet Desperation

At the post office he sees Joe McInnes.
Joe says. "We're having some people over.
It'll be informal. Come as you are."

She is in the middle
of preparing dinner. Tonight
she is trying an experiment:
Hal Burgonyaual—Fish-Potato Casserole.
She has cooked and drained the potatoes
and cut the fish in pieces.
Now she has to "mash potatoes,
add butter and hot millk," et cetera.

He relays Joe's invitation.
"No," she says, "not on your life.
Muriel McInnes is no friend of mine."

It appears that she told Muriel
that the Goldins live above their means,
and Muriel told Mary Goldin.

He listens carefully, to get things right.
The feud between the Andersons and the Kellys
began with Ruth Anderson calling Mike Kelly
a reckless driver. Finally
the Andersons had to sell their house and move.

Social life is no joke.
It can be the only life there is.

*

In the living room the battle of Iwo Jima
is in progress, watched by his son.

Men are dying on the beach,
pinned down by a machine gun.

The marine carrying the satchel charge
falls. Then Sergeant Stryker
picks up the charge and starts running.

Now you are with the enemy machine gun
firing out of the pillbox
as Stryker comes running,
bullets at his heels kicking up dust.
He makes it to the base of the pillbox,
lights the charge, raises up,
and heaves it through the opening.
The pillbox explodes . . .
the NCO's wave, "Move out!"

And he rises to his feet.
He's seen the movie. Stryker gets killed
just as they're raising the flag.

                    *

A feeling of pressure . . .
There is something that needs to be done
immediately.

            But there is nothing,
only himself. His life is passing,
and afterwards there will be eternity,
silence, and infinite space.

He thinks, Firewood!—
and goes to the basement,
takes the Swede saw off the wall,
and goes outside, to the woodpile.

He carries an armful to the sawhorse
and saws the logs into smaller pieces.
In twenty minutes he has a pile of firewood
cut just the right length.
He carries the cut logs into the house
and arranges them in a neat pile
next to the fireplace.

Then looks around for something else to do,
to relieve the feeling of pressure.

The dog!
He will take the dog for a walk.

*

They make a futile procession . . .
he commanding her to "Heel!"—
she dragging back or straining ahead.

The leaves are turning yellow.
Between the trunks of the trees
the cove is blue, with ripples.
The swans—this year there are seven—
are sailing line astern.

But when you come closer
the rocks above the shore are littered
with daggers of broken glass
where the boys sat on summer nights
and broke beer bottles afterwards.

And the beach is littered,
with cans, containers, heaps of garbage,
newspaper wadded against the sea-wall.
Someone has even dumped a mattress . . .
a definite success!

Some daring guy, some Stryker
in the pickup speeding away.

He cannot bear the sun
going over and going down . . .
the trees and houses vanishing
in quiet every day.

The Previous Tenant

1

All that winter it snowed.
The sides of roads were heaped with it.
The nights were quiet. If you stepped outside,
above the dark woods and fields
hung glittering stars and constellations.

My landlord, Stanley, came by now and then
to see how things were going.
I reminded him that the previous tenant
had left boxes full of clothes,
a pair of skis, a rifle,
three shelves of books, and a fishing pole.

All right, he said, he'd get in touch with him.
I said, he must have left in a hurry.

A hurry? Stanley considered.
His eyes gleamed under bushy eyebrows.
Satanic. But I happened to know that Stanley
wouldn't hurt a fly. All that Fall
I'd seen him trying to think of something
to persuade some raccoons to quit the premises—
everything short of a gun.

"McNeil was a bit disorganized,"
he said with a smile.

I asked if he'd like some coffee,
and he said yes. While I was making it
he talked about the previous tenant.

2

A doctor named Hugh McNeil
came on the staff at Mercy Hospital
and bought a house in Point Mercy.

Hugh and Nancy fitted right in . . .
people liked them.
Helen Knox, whose husband was vice-president
of the National Maritime Bank,
called on Nancy and invited her
to join the Garden Club.
Then they were asked to join the Golf Club.
(The Levines, on the other hand, hadn't been invited.
After two years of Point Mercy
they sold their house and moved back to Queens.)

The McNeils had children: Tom, fourteen,
and Laurie, nine and a half, nearly ten.
McNeil was one of the fathers on Saturday
dashing about. He drove a green Land Rover
as though he were always on safari
with the children and an Irish setter.

Nancy was nice . . . blonde,
and intelligent—she'd been to Wellesley.
She took on the job of secretary
of the Garden Club, that nobody wanted,
and helped organize the dance at the Yacht Club
on July the Fourth, for Hugh had joined that too.
He bought a "Cal" Thirty Martini-rigged sloop,
and with Tom as crew went sailing.
They came in fifth in the Martha Woodbury
Perpetual Trophy.

                    Nancy didn't sail,
it made her seasick. She sat on the patio

with her knitting till the boats hove in sight,
then went down to the basin.

McNeil spoke at village meetings
with moderation and common sense.
Once he argued for retaining
the Latin teacher at the high school.
Latin, he explained, was still useful
for medicine and law, and a foundation
for good English. They heard him out
and voted to let the Latin teacher go
and remodel the gymnasium.
McNeil accepted defeat gracefully.
That was one of the things they liked about him.

The residents of Point Mercy
are proud of their village
with its beautiful homes and gardens
and wild life sanctuary.
Contrary to what people say
about the suburbs, they appreciate culture.
Hugh McNeil was an example . . .
doing the shopping, going to the club,
a man in no way different from themselves,
husband and family man
and good neighbor, who nevertheless spoke Latin.

3

Her name was Irene Davis.
Before she married it was Cristiano.
"I met her once," said Helen Knox.
"Harry introduced her to me
at the bank. A dark woman . . .
I think, a touch of the tar brush."

There is no accounting for tastes
observed Sandie Bishop.

The woman's husband was an invalid
and patient of Dr. McNeil.
The green Land Rover had been seen
parked outside the Davis house
in the afternoon, in the evening, and once—
this was hilarious—the doctor
ran out of gas in that part of town
at three in the morning. He didn't have cash
or credit cards on him, and had to walk
to the nearest open service station.
The attendant let him have a gallon.
" I've been in the same fix," he told McNeil,
"you can pay me some other time."

The attendant talked, and the story
got back to Point Mercy.
"It's a scandal," said Sandie.
"Do you think Nancy knows?"
Helen said, "I'm sure she does."

"Someone should have a talk with him,"
Sandie said. She remembered
with some excitement, the occasion
when a resident of Point Mercy
had been thinking of selling his house
to a family that was black.
Every morning he would find garbage
dumped on his lawn. The prospective buyer
received an anonymous letter,
and that was the end of that.

"Let's not be hasty," said Helen
who was president of the Garden Club
and had more experience.
"These things have a way of working themselves out."

4

One day there was a sensation:
Dr. McNeil had been mugged,
beaten and left by the road.

"Mugged?" said the service station attendant.
This was long after the event.

He looked around, but there was no one
in hearing distance, only the dog,
a hound that wandered around
with an infected ear, snapping at flies.
All at once it perked up its ears
and went running. It must have smelled something
mixed with the odor of gasoline
and dust . . . a delirious
fragrance of sensual life.

The attendant leaned closer
and said in a conspiratorial voice,
"He was never mugged.
It was Irene Davis's brothers,
the Cristianos. They had him beat up."

He knew about gangsters. They would beat up a guy
to warn him. The next time it was curtains.

5

So McNeil was in the hospital
with two broken ribs, black eyes,
and a missing tooth.

At the next meeting of the Garden Club
the president said she was as broad-minded

as anyone, but this . . .
here she paused as though it were beneath her
to find words for such low behavior . . .
had brought violence into their midst.

Sandie moved they send a delegation
to the hospital, to demand
McNeil's immediate resignation.

The next day four of the members
called on Dr. Abrahams, chief of staff,
and told him what they wanted.
A short man, with hair on his face,
all the time they were talking he kept turning
from one to the other, and grinning
like some sort of monkey,
Sandie said afterwards.

He thanked them for their concern.
But McNeil's private life—
not that he knew anything about it—
had nothing to do with his work
or his position here at the hospital.
If they would take his advice
they would be careful what they said—
they might find themselves charged
with libel. Speaking, he was sure,
for the entire staff, they were fortunate
to have a surgeon of Hugh McNeil's caliber.

Could he be of service in anything else?
No? Then would they please excuse him . . .
it looked like a busy day.

They were halfway to the parking lot.
"What can you expect?" said Helen.
"It was bad enough letting them in,
but to make one chief of staff!"

She knew how to put what they were feeling
into words. This was why
she was president—elected not once
or twice . . . this was her third term in office.

6

Then Nancy sued for divorce.
She had all the evidence she needed:
her husband had been with Irene Davis
in Providence, Rhode Island,
when he was supposed to be in Boston
attending a medical conference.

This was when he moved into the cottage.
It consisted of a small bedroom,
living room, bathroom, kitchen.
Thoreau, who recommends sleeping in the box
railroad workers keep their tools in,
would have found this house commodious.

I could imagine him coming home . . .
putting some fries on a metal sheet
and sliding it into the oven
set at 350 degrees.
Sprinkling a couple of chops
with pepper and garlic.
Deciding which frozen vegetable . . .
say, spinach. Putting the block
in a saucer with water and salt.
Making a salad . . . but this would mean
slicing tomatoes, radishes, scallions,
and washing lettuce. There would be times
when he just couldn't be bothered.

He would have a drink, then a second.
You have to be careful not to make it three

and four. On the other hand
you shouldn't be too careful,
or like Robinson Crusoe you may find yourself
taking pride in the neatness and efficiency
of your domestic arrangements:
all your bowls made out of gourds
lined up on a shelf according to size.
Ditto your spoons.
"A place for everything," you say to the parrot,
"and everything in its place."

Bake the French fries,
boil the frozen vegetable, broil the lamb chops.
You can prepare a nourishing dinner
in twenty minutes, and eat it in five
while reading the *Times* or watching *Charlie's Angels*.

He would watch TV again after dinner.
My God, he'd say to the walls,
it can't be this bad. But it was.
He'd turn it off and pick up a book.
Now that he had plenty of time
he could catch up on the ones he'd missed
when they came out: titles like *Future Shock*
and *The Greening of America*.

Then he was on an express train
racing to the end of the line,
a flash and a moment of excruciating
pain. He was paralyzed,
helpless to move a leg or an arm.

And woke, having fallen asleep
in his chair, to hear the dripping
of snow melting on the roof.

On nights when he couldn't sleep
he'd watch the late late show.

In the dark night of the soul,
says F. Scott Fitzgerald,
it is always three in the morning.
Hemingway says, it isn't so bad . . .
in fact, the best hour of the night
once you've reconciled yourself to insomnia
and stopped worrying about your sins.
And I say that insomnia can be
a positive joy if you're tuned into *Dames*
or *Gold Diggers of 1933*.
I remember seeing *The Producers*
at three in the morning and practically
falling out of bed. There are pleasures
known to none but late late movie-goers,
moments of the purest absurdity,
such as, in an otherwise boring movie
starring the Marx Brothers, the "Tenement Symphony"
as sung by Tony Martin.

So there he was, watching Busby Berkeley's
electrically lighted waterfalls,
and the Warner Brothers cuties
viewed from underneath, treading water.

"Ain't we got fun!" shrieked the parrot,
and the goat gave a great bound.

7

Behind the Perry Masons and Agatha Christies
I came across a packet of letters.
It was like being a detective.

When Irene's husband came home
from the hospital, he was confined
to his bed, by doctor's orders.
And McNeil was the doctor.

"Call me at home," said Irene.
"There is no problem about telephone calls."

I copied some of the passages—
they might come in useful.
There was an idea for a novel
I'd had for years: *A Bovary of the Sierras* . . .
The Bovary of Evanston . . . The Bovary of Green Harbor.
There was a paragraph about some flowers
and his cock that might have been conceived
by the author of *Lady Chatterley's Lover.*
It went to show that when an idea
has genuine merit, individuals
far removed in space and time
come upon it independently.

She even knew her Bible:
"When my beloved slipped his hand through the latch-hole
my bowels stirred within me."

Rumor was right. It was her brothers
who had McNeil beaten up.
She told him that he wasn't to see her
ever again. She feared for his life.
"Irene . . . signing off."

But she didn't sign off. Here she was again.
"If you have a new woman in your life
or you've gone back to your wife
I don't want to muck things up.
This is just a peacepipe, kid—
send me a smoke signal
if I'm getting in the way of anything.
Cheerio, Irene."

Then they picked up again where they'd left off.
They had been with each other yesterday.
She could still feel him inside her.

I was beginning to be afraid
for him. For her. For both of them.

8

Stanley telephoned to say that McNeil
was coming to pick up his things.

I put the books in cartons,
and piled the cartons and the rest of his things
next to the door: the boxes of clothes,
the skis, the fishing pole,
and the rifle—I was loath to part with it,
the way America was greening.

The next day my predecessor
arrived. A man of forty
with red hair . . . looking slightly angry.
Suspicious. I couldn't put my finger on it.

He was accompanied by a young woman
wearing jeans and a sweater.
She was fair, and had a friendly smile.
"It was good of you to take care
of Hugh's things," she said. "Wasn't it, Hugh?"
"O yes," he said. "Thanks."

I helped them carry things out
to the station wagon. It was snowing again . . .
not flakes but particles, coming down fast
at an angle, like rain or hail.

They drove away.
She waved. He looked straight ahead.
It appeared he was back on the track
once more, after his derailment.

With a woman of the right kind at his side
to give him a nudge. "Say thanks!"

9

It is always that famous day and year
at the Colony Inn . . . a brick fireplace,
rough-hewn beams, and pewter candlesticks.
From the ceiling hang the flags
of the thirteen original colonies.

The waitresses wear bonnets and muslin gowns
that hang straight from the shoulder
to the floor, leaving their arms and elbows
exposed. Some of the older waitresses
seem to resent being made to dress
like children. Their movements are slow.

One of them arrived finally
to take our order and departed,
moving with slow steps
as befitted an early American.

Maggie said, "Don't look now!
By the window . . . that's Irene Davis,
the woman McNeil had the affair with."

I looked around the room casually
and let my gaze come to rest
on Irene.

They said she was dark. What they hadn't said
was that the darkness, jet black hair,
was set off by a skin like snow,
like moonlight in a dark field.
Her features were . . . fine. She wouldn't have been

out of place in an Italian villa
with walls five feet thick, and chickens
roosting on the furniture . . . the family
crowded into three rooms upstairs . . .
a *contessa,* married to the invalid son
of impoverished aristocracy.

I wondered what she would have thought
if she'd known I'd read her letters.

There were two people with her:
an old woman with white hair
who looked as though she'd just got off
the boat from Palermo . . .
and a man, he must be Irene's brother . . .
the same black hair and white complexion.
But what in her looked romantic,
in him spelled murder. He was thin
and sinewy . . . wearing a green jacket,
dark green shirt, white tie.

I imagined he was being tolerant
of the restaurant . . . these assholes
with their consommés and casseroles,
their salads consisting of lettuce and
cottage cheese. And what was this
for chrissake? Sweet potato
with marshmallow on top . . . you call this food?

But he was on his best behavior.
He didn't pull an automatic
and blow holes through the flags
of the thirteen original colonies.

Irene must have felt me staring.
She turned . . . her eyes met mine
for a few seconds. I had an impression
of . . . defiance. "What do you want?"

I quickly looked away.

10

Maggie was meeting a friend
at three. It was now two-thirty.
So we walked around Island Bay.

The village has been reconstructed
to preserve a Colonial atmosphere.
At the crest of a slope facing the bay
stands the post office. This at least
is authentic. It has four columns,
white of course, and a big golden eagle
above the entrance. On either side
in a crescent there are shops
with signs lettered in gold:
Optometrist, Pharmacy, Antiques . . .
There's a shop selling Irish linen
and wool. Another selling jewelry
and notions . . . Royal Doulton . . .
little statues of Colonial women
in hoopskirts and wigs,
and the figure of a young girl
in shorts, taking a swing at a golf ball.

The slope goes down to a road.
Between this and the bay
stands a gazebo, an open dome
housing a bust of Hercules.
This, they say, was a ship's figurehead.
All but the bearded head
is a reconstruction . . . some local artist
has added a muscular torso
and draped over one shoulder
the skin of the Nemean lion.
A sillier, more pathetic monster

it would be hard to imagine,
with his doggy nose and wide-open eyes
that seem to say, Look at me.
I never did any harm.

This monument to our culture,
believe it or not, had been vandalized . . .
battered and gashed.
Whoever did it must have used a hammer
or an axe.

I said, "Boys will be boys."

"I'm sure," Maggie said, "it wasn't anyone
from around here."

I wasn't so sure. Our high schools
every year turn out their quota of vandals
and thieves. Not to mention illiterates.
You don't have to go into New York City . . .

How, she said, could I be so cynical?

I said, why was it that when you told the truth
people accused you of being cynical?

We were on our way to having a quarrel.
I didn't want to. I liked Maggie,
with her quizzical way of looking at me,
her air of calm, unclouded judgment,
her mouth that turned down at one corner
when she smiled.

But now she wasn't smiling.
She said, "It's your attitude.
Like what you said in the restaurant
about Hugh McNeil and the Davis woman
being better than the rest of us."

She had her back to the post office.
The wings of the golden eagle
seemed to spring out of her shoulders.

I was filled with a sense of the ridiculous.
She sensed it, and became really angry.
"I know, you prefer vulgar people.
Anyone who tries to be decent and respectable
is either a hypocrite or a fool."

So we had our quarrel.
Then a car drove up and stopped.
It was Helen Knox. She leaned over
and opened the door for Maggie.

"Good afternoon," she said to me,
very cool. I knew what she thought of me
and my writing. A friend told me—
for writers have such friends.

She said, "I thought I ought to read
one of his novels. But I couldn't bring myself
to finish it. Why write about
such ordinary things?

What with chauffeuring the children
and entertaining Harry's friends,
if I find time to read, it has to be something
that takes me out of myself.

You have to be selective—
this is why I read *The New Yorker,* and *Time*
and subscribe to the Book of the Month."

The Eleventh Commandment

"Do you know the eleventh commandment?"
Harry asks. I shake my head.
I'm the straight man in these encounters.

"The eleventh commandment,"
he says, "is, 'Don't get caught.'"

Then, as I recall, everyone laughs.

*

He hands a hundred-dollar bill
to his older boy, to buy fireworks
from a man from New Jersey
who's selling them out of his truck.

Then he and I and the boys
are setting them off. Rockets
go climbing with a whoosh
and bang! The sky above Green Harbor
is lit red, white, and blue.
Bright flares come glimmering down.
People have come out of their houses
and stand in the street, looking up.

A thoroughly illegal operation
that everyone is taking part in . . .
What could be more appropriate
on the Fourth of July? More American?

*

If you want to accomplish anything
in this world, you can't be too particular.

Ethics are nice to have on a wall, in Latin,
but Latin won't meet a payroll.
And don't give me any of that
about the system. It's the same in Russia.

*

When the financial scandal burst
in the light of the flash he was still smiling,
"confident that he and his partners
would be cleared of all violations"—

kickbacks, misapplication of funds,
conspiracy, fraud, concealment, wire fraud,
falsified books and records, and
interstate transportation of stolen property.

*

"I miss him," she says.

"What makes me sick
is the way everyone's turned against him.

Let me tell you about the people
next door. They're stealing bricks
from a building site. Every night
they drive over and steal some more.
They're making a patio and an outdoor barbecue."

Her younger boy, Kyle, comes over
and stands watchfully in front of me.
He is wearing a spaceman's helmet
and carrying a ray gun or laser.

"Hi there," I say to him.
What else do you say to a six-year-old?

Periodontics

"Am I hurting you?" says Eubie.
I shake my head, no,
for I've learned not to show pain.
At the school of dental hygiene
where Eubie got her diploma
they teach them not to be put off
by a wince or gathering tear
but to stay on the sensitive spot
and "Festina lente". . . be thorough.

I try to think of something else . . .
"P.C." The initials
on the dental unit in front of me.

These were Paula's initials.
The Chapmans lived on Riverside Drive
obliquely across from the sign
for Spry. "Spry for Baking"
it said, and blinked off,
then on again. "For Frying."

The apartment had wall-to-wall carpeting
and dark brown furniture waxed so it shone.
There was a cabinet with glass doors
full of objets d'art: an elephant
carved out of ivory, a wooden Russian doll.
There was an old windup Victrola
with hits from Broadway musicals
and "classics," Gershwin and Tchaikovsky.
A bookcase held *The Wandering Jew* by Eugene Sue.

Mr. Chapman had studied for the Ph.D.
but universities wouldn't hire a Jew
so instead he went into business.

"How are we doing?" says Eubie.
 OK, I nod, fine.
I call her my Buchenwald Baby . . .
with her eyes of cornflower blue
that never look into mine
directly, but at some view
slightly to the right or to the left
as she travels with the cavitron.

*

"Oh my God," said Paula,
"he isn't even wearing a tie!"

She looked like a fairy princess
in a bright blue gown
that showed that her breasts
had budded, as Proust would say.

I was wearing a suit
but it was brown and tired.
And I had no tie . . .
I hadn't thought it was required.

"He can wear one of your father's,"
said Mrs. Chapman.

So we went to the prom after all
where Paula danced with everyone else.
As I stood by the wall drinking quantities
of pink lemonade out of paper cups
her laughter rang like a chime of bells.

*

I didn't see her for years
while I was in the army.

Then we made up for lost time
at the movies, in the balcony,
on my sofa that converted into a bed . . .
and under the trees—it was summer—
at night on Riverside Drive.

"Spry for Baking" said the sign
shining above the Palisades.
A barge with its warning lights
would be going up the Hudson . . .
the George Washington Bridge
gleaming in the moonlight
against the scudding clouds.
"That's it," said Paula. "There."

*

"Are you all right?" says Eubie.
I nod. I'm not going to let on.
Though I brush after every meal,
when she gives me the paper cup
with the liquid that's bright red
and bitter . . . and I have held it in my mouth
for thirty seconds, spat it out,
and rinsed with the mouthwash,
and she hands me the mirror,
there are always some traces
of the plaque that causes decay.

*

Mrs. Chapman didn't approve of me.
It took me some time to catch on.
"He's too," she told Paula, "bohemian."

She was saving her precious daughter
for someone able to provide her

with the better things of life:
wall-to-wall carpeting and dark brown furniture.

Paula wanted to "be in the theater."
So her mother packed her off
to some second-rate school in Boston
where they taught it . . . whatever it was.

Actors, I told her, weren't people.
Like monkeys or parrots
they could repeat sounds and simulate feelings
but had none of their own.

"Don't call me," she said, "I'll call you."

*

She was as good as her word . . .
she called, twenty years later.
She had just "winged in" from the Coast
and was staying at a friend's apartment
in Soho. There was a restaurant
right on the corner.

I recognized her at once
though she was wearing a pants suit
and big glasses with rhinestones,
and the skin that used to look like
some marvelous tropical fruit
was sallow . . . and the glossy black hair
was still black, but lusterless like ink.

The expressions that used to be endearing . . .
fluttering her eyelashes,
touching her tongue to her top lip,
were like the moving eyelids and mouth
of a doll.

And the shop talk!
She kept dropping names
of people in Hollywood and Beverly Hills
I'd never heard of or wanted to.

I said as much. I could hear myself
sneering, like Diogenes in a washtub.
And what did I have to feel so
superior about?
Where were my screen credits?
Did I own a swimming pool?

More to the point . . .
where was the novel I was going to write
that would put Proust in the shade?

*

The magic, as they say, was gone,
like a song that used to be on the hit parade.

But there is always a new song,
and some things never change.
Not long ago, visiting a friend
who lives on Riverside Drive
I saw that the sign for Spry
is still there, shining away.

"Spry for Baking." It blinks off
and on again . . . "For Frying."
Then the lights run around in a circle.

Ed

Ed was in love with a cocktail waitress,
but Ed's family, and his friends,
didn't approve. So he broke it off.

He married a respectable woman
who played the piano. She played well enough
to have been a professional.

Ed's wife left him. . . .
Years later, at a family gathering
Ed got drunk and made a fool of himself.

He said, "I should have married Doreen."
"Well," they said, "why didn't you?"

Akhmatova's Husband

Akhmatova's husband, Gumilev,
was a poet and an explorer.
He wrote poems about wild animals
and had fantastic ideas:
a red bird with the head of a girl
and a lost tram that goes wandering,

shedding fire "like a storm with dark wings,"
passing over bridges,
by a house with three windows
where a woman he loved once lived,
and, rushing toward him,
two raised hooves and an iron glove.

Gumilev fought in the Great War
with almost incredible valor,
twice winning the Cross of Saint George.
He envisioned a little old man
forging the bullet that would kill him.

It wasn't a German bullet, it was Russian.
Gumilev was killed by his own countrymen
as poets in Russia frequently are.

Everyone talks about Akhmatova
but no one talks about Gumilev.
That wouldn't have mattered to Gumilev.
When the man from the government came to kill him,
"Just give me a cigarette," said Gumilev,
"and let's get it over with."

Reflections in a Spa

The walls are lines with mirrors,
doubling their images, front and back.
You see yourself receding in a tunnel.

The man on the adjacent bicycle
speaks: "Whakunam?"
Finally I understand: he has no voice box.
"Whakunam?" means "What's your name?"
"Amjaw"—"I am George."

There are impressive physical specimens:
body builders, weight lifters
with limbs of oak, bellies ridged like washboards.
On the other hand, some whose doctors
have said, "Exercise, or else!"

And some like George, and a night watchman
whose legs are withered and walks
dragging each foot across the floor,
like a "partially destroyed insect!"
—the cripple Doyle in *Miss Lonelyhearts*.

The time will pass more easily
thinking about *Miss Lonelyhearts*.
Without fiction life would be hell.

I feel like a disembodied spirit.
Who is that balding middle-aged man
in the mirror, pedaling away from me?
Strange, the back of one's own head
and body growing small.

In a Time of Peace

He changes dollars into francs
and walks, from Rue de Rivoli
almost to the Arc de Triomphe.

He sits at a sidewalk café
and looks at the ones who are passing.
Then goes to a restaurant
and a show.

       Someone told him the Crazy Horse
is the place to go, "un spectacle de deux heures"
you can understand "if you're Javanese,
dead drunk, or mentally retarded."
There are sketches, stripteases:
blonde Solange, black Marianne,
Ingrid with her boots and whip . . .
and who can forget Duzia,
"the most wanted girl in Europe"?

The chorus in the entr'actes
jump and squeal. Imagining
their own nudity is driving them mad.

After the show he chooses to walk.
The lamps in leafy avenues
shining on monuments and statues . . .

       *

A sea of amethyst is breaking
along two miles of beach umbrellas . . .
the car parks, red roofs
of the bathing establishments,

Lidino, Antaura . . . advertisements
for Stock, Coca-Cola,
"tutte le Sera DISCOTECA."

A child on the crowded sand
is playing with a new toy.
It hurls an object into the air,
a parachute opens, it descends . . .
homunculus, a little plastic man
returning from Outer Space.

Some day we may have to live there,
but for the present life consists
of sex . . . all the beautiful bodies
that you see on the beach:
food—there are dozens of places,
ranging from the ice-cream parlor
to Tito's—Ristorante Tito del Molo;
things to buy: Galletti for handbags,
Timpano for a lighter;
and entertainment: the Cinema Odeon,
the bar with pinball machines.
There is even a Sauna Finlandese.

At night the promenade glitters,
loud music fills the air.
Not good music . . . but it doesn't matter
to the families with small children
or to the lovers.

The Unwritten Poem

You will never write the poem about Italy.
What Socrates said about love
is true of poetry—where is it?
Not in beautiful faces and distant scenery
but the one who writes and loves.

In your life here, on this street
where the houses from the outside
are all alike, and so are the people.
Inside, the furniture is dreadful—
flock on the walls, and huge color television.

To love and write unrequited
is the poet's fate. Here you'll need
all your ardor and ingenuity.
This is the front and these are the heroes—
a life beginning with "Hi!" and ending with "So long!"

You must rise to the sound of the alarm
and march to catch the 6:20—
watch as they ascend the station platform
and, grasping briefcases, pass beyond your gaze
and hurl themselves into the flames.

from
IN THE ROOM WE SHARE

1990
✳

Riverside Drive

I have been staring at a sentence
for fifteen minutes. The mind
was not made for social science.

I take my overcoat and go.

Night has fallen on Riverside Drive . . .
the sign for Spry shining
across the Hudson: "Spry for Frying****
for Baking."

I am thinking of Rilke
and "Who if I cried would hear me
among the angelic orders?"

It seems that we are here to say
names like "Spry" and "Riverside Drive" . . .
to carry the names of places
and things with us, into the night

glimmering with stars and constellations.

Numbers and Dust

All day we were training in dust.
At night we returned to barracks
worn out, too tired to say anything.

On weekends we traveled long distances
to Fort Worth, Austin, San Antonio,
looking for excitement, walking up and down
with all the other enlisted men,
trying to pick up a shop girl
or waitress hurrying home.

No luck that way, so we'd split up
and agree to meet back at the depot.

           *

Now you're by yourself, on Vine Street
or Magnolia, gazing at sprinklers,
a bicycle lying in the drive.

A curtain moves as you pass . . . some old lady.

Then there are bigger houses, with lawns and gardens:
English Tudor, a French château,
Bauhaus. The rich like to shop around.

           *

I am a guest years later
in one of those houses.

                    Looking through a window
at some trees, I ask their names.

"Flowering judas, golden rain tree,
ceniza . . . that's very Texan."

And the birds picking at berries?
Waxwings. They get drunk, she says.

In the room behind me Isaac Singer
is talking about golems, things like men
created out of numbers and dust.

*

Two rabbis once made a golem
and sent it to Rabbi Zera
who tried to engage it in conversation.
But the golem spoke not a word.
Finally he said, "You must have been made
by the numbers. Return to your dust."

I think I can see one now,
standing by the gate,
in the uniform of an enlisted man.

It stands looking up at me
for a few moments, then turns away
in silence, returning to dust.

Another Boring Story

Chekhov has "A Boring Story"
about a professor.
The old man's wife and children
don't understand him and don't care.

His wife's only concern is
to marry off their daughter
to this blockhead, a nonentity.
So the old man goes on a journey
to investigate, find out what he can
about their future son-in-law . . .
and finds himself in a hotel room
in a strange town, wondering
how on earth life brought him there.

He has a friend, a young woman.
They're not lovers . . . loving friends.
She had an affair that turned sour
and now she's at loose ends.
She asks him what to do, what to live for,
and he has nothing to say to her,
not a word. That's the end of the story.

Here's another boring story about a professor.
Years ago he embarked on an affair
with a young woman. It became a scandal.
His wife threw him out,
then she took him back. The young woman
tried to kill herself, I'm told.

I see them fairly often.
He and I talk about literature
and what's wrong with the country
while his wife knits or does some ironing.

I find myself looking out the window
or at the walls. Some surrealist
recommends staring at a wall
till something unusual happens . . .
an arm protruding from the wall.

He mixes drinks, she lays out cheese-dip.
Then the children come running in,
streaked with dirt from wherever they've been.
They make for the cheese-dip,
stick their fingers in and dabble.

I've seen them at the table.
They snatch the meat from the plate
with their hands.

She smiles at her little savages.
One thing's sure: she's not raising her children
to be members of any faculty.

The People Next Door

He isn't a religious man.
So instead of going to church
on Sunday they go to sea.

They cruise up and down,
see the ferry coming from Bridgeport
to Green Harbor, and going back
from Green Harbor to Bridgeport . . .
and all the boats there are.
The occasional silent fisherman . . .
When the kids start to get restless
he heads back to shore.

I hear them returning
worn out and glad to be home.
This is as close to being happy
as a family ever gets.
I envy their content. And yet
I've done that too, and know
that no hobby or activity
distracts one from thinking
forever. Every human being
is an intellectual more or less.

I too was a family man.
It was a phase I had to go through.
I remember tenting in the Sierras,
getting up at dawn to fly cast.
I remember my young son
almost being blown off the jetty
in Lochalsh. Only the suitcase
he was carrying held him down.
The same, at Viareggio,

followed me into the sea
and was almost swept away by the current.

These are the scenes I recall
rather than Christmas and Thanksgiving.
My life as the father of a family
seems to have been a series
of escapes, not to mention illnesses,
confrontations with teachers,
administrators, police.
Flaubert said, "They're in the right,"
looking at a bourgeois family,
and then went back happily
to his dressing gown and pipe.

Yes, I believe in the family . . .
next door. I rejoice
at their incomings and outgoings.
I am present when Betty
goes out on her first date.
I hear about Joey's being chosen
for the team. I survive the takeover
of the business, and the bad scare
at the doctor's.
I laugh with them that laugh
and mourn with them that mourn.

I see their lights, and hear a murmur
of voices from house to house.

It gives me a strange feeling
to think how far they've come
from some far world to this,
bending their necks to the yoke
of affection.

And that one day,

with a few simple words
and flowers to keep them company
they'll return once more to the silence
out there, beyond the stars.

White Oxen

A man walks beside them
with a whip that he cracks.
The cart they draw is painted
with Saracens and Crusaders,
fierce eyes and ranks of spears.

They are on the steep road
that goes up the mountain.
Their neat-stepping hoofs
appear to be flickering
in the sun, raising dust.

They are higher than the roofs
on which striped gourds and melons
lie ripening. They move
among the dark green olives
that grow on the rocks.

They dwindle as they climb . . .
vanish around a corner
and reappear walking on the edge
of a precipice. They enter
the region of mist and darkness.

I think I can see them still:
a pair of yoked oxen
the color of ivory
or smoke, with red tassels,
in the gathering dusk.

Waiting in the Service Station

Waiting in the service station,
reading *Sports Illustrated,*

listening to every sound
and wondering, is it mine? . . .

When they say the car is ready
and I go to pay the bill

I'm relieved, I'd pay anything
to be out of there, on the road,

moving with the traffic,
looking at the buildings and signs:

Clams 'n Stuff, Scelfo Realty,
Candi's X-Rated Dancers.

A Bramble Bush

One night in winter Willa went missing.
I took my Irish raincoat, gloves,
and a flashlight.

          In half an hour
I had her and the wood had me,
caught in brambles. I couldn't use my hands—
if I set her down she'd run off again.

So I stood there, seeing the irony,
lights only a hundred yards away,
and hearing sounds of television:
the murmur of a voice, or voices,
followed by a roar of applause . . .
some situation comedy or stand-up comedian.

      *

Winter has passed, and it is spring again
when the small green buds with forked tails
like fishes swim on the wind.
Then summer, gold on green . . .
Looking at the sky through the leaves
is like looking through shining crystal.

Then the leaves come drifting down,
and it's December. Frau Holle
fills the sky with white feathers.
Rain falls and freezes. The boughs are sheathed
in ice, with bright icicles hanging down
like lace. The whole wood glitters.

      *

After some prolonged litigation
between the Town and the man who owns the land
the wood stands on, it has been agreed
to cut the trees down and build houses.
The development is to be called Birchwood
and zoned for half or quarter acres.

And so, one spring, comes the surveyor
squinting through his telescope. "Joe,"
he shouts, "look behind you!
What's that in the bush?"

                        Joe looks and sees,
tangled in thorns, the skeleton of a man
still holding the skeleton of a dog.

                   *

A cold gust of air set the wood rustling.
Lightning flashed. There was a roll of thunder.
But this was not my kind of story.
I turned around with my back to the brambles
and, holding the dog to my chest,
hurled myself backward.

They gave a little. I did it again . . .
and so, standing and falling, made lunatic progress
until I fell out of a bush into the open.

I rested a while, then put her on the leash,
and walked the short way home, arriving
as the first cold raindrops fell.

Sea of Grass

For Jimmy Ernst

If you're a Jew and want to know
which transport your mother was on,
the French railroads have a list.
Jimmy showed me the name of his:
"Lou Straus-Ernst . . . Transport 76."

One of those who made the journey
and survived, gave an account:
"Seventy would be put in a boxcar.
There would be a long wait
while the train was boarded up.
Then three days' travel east . . .
paper mattresses on the floor
for the sick, bare boards for the rest.
Many did not survive."

*

At Auschwitz shortly before the end
one had seen her: "A woman totally exhausted,
half lying, half leaning against a wall,
warming herself in the last rays of a dying sun."

And still we believe in loving-kindness . . .
some even believe there's a God.
This is a mystery, *ein Rätsel*
God himself could not explain.

*

A few minutes' walk from the house
where I live, there's a beach,

a brown strip of sand
lined with tide-wrack and litter . . .
boards, plastic bottles
and, at the water's edge, green reeds.

"Sea of Grass" Jimmy called it.
Every time I come here I think of him
and his painting.

       "Work!
God wants you to," said Flaubert.

There they are every summer
just as he painted them,
growing up again . . . a hedge
of stems and leaves standing motionless.

Blue water, and a harbor's mouth
opening into the sky.

from
THERE YOU ARE

1995
✳

The Choir Master's Evening Party

Mr. Cooper, the physics teacher,
was a cross-eyed little Englishman.
When he was angry he reddened
and shouted and spit flew.
He was also in charge of the choir
and would have us to his house.
We sang "The Londonderry Air,"
"What shall we do with the drunken sailor?"
and a song with the refrain,
"Oh no John, no John, no John, no!"
which was daring. Then Mrs. Cooper
who wore black ankle boots
came in and gave us tea and biscuits.

The evening came to an end
with a song about a dying swan,
and we walked back across the commons.
The moon stared through a window
on rows of beds. No talking
after "lights out." The diesel
labored in the night. The house master
coughed in his study. I lay
and listened to the roof beams creaking
in the wind from across the sea.

Suddenly

Nipkow and Cosulich
exported "seconds," merchandise
with small imperfections . . .
nylon stockings, ballpoint pens.
I packed them in cellophane,
then cartons, to be shipped
to Europe for their postwar legs
and literary movements.

Nipkow had a sideline, diamonds
He would sit at his desk by the hour
holding a diamond up to the light
or staring at some little diamonds
in the palm of his left hand.
He'd rise and grind a diamond
on the wheel. Then put on his coat
and go to meet someone like himself
with whom he would exchange diamonds,
each of them making a profit
somehow out of this.

One day I suddenly quit.
Then I worked on the *Herald Tribune*.
A reporter would call "Copyboy!"
and one of us would run over
and take his copy to the horseshoe
where the Count, as we named him,
a bald head and rimless glasses,
presided over his crew.

One would read the piece in a hurry
and write a heading for it,
so many letters to fit.

My greatest adventure
was going to the fourteenth floor
of the Waldorf Astoria
to fetch copy about the flower show
at Madison Square Garden.

I quit that job suddenly too.
"You didn't like the export business,"
said Sylvia Cosulich—
I was still seeing her
though her parents didn't approve—
"and you don't want to be a reporter.
What are you going to do?"

In the silence there were sounds
of the traffic down below,
the elevator opening.

               Suddenly
the room seemed far away.
I was looking through a window
at clouds and trees.

And looking down again
to write, as I am now.

Al and Beth

My Uncle Al worked in a drugstore
three blocks above Times Square,
dispensing pills and cosmetics.
All day long crazy people
and thieves came into the store,
but nothing seemed to faze him.

His sister, Beth, was the opposite . . .
romantic. She used to sing
on ships that sailed from New York
to Central and South America.
When the tourists came trailing back
on board with their maracas,
Beth would be in the Aztec Room
singing "Smoke Gets in Your Eyes"
and "I Get a Kick out of You."

Once when I argued with Al
about something that America
was doing . . . "My country
right or wrong," he told me.
I suppose so, if you've come
from a village in Russia no one
ever heard of, with no drains,
and on saints' days the Cossacks
descend on you with the blessing
of the Church, to beat out your brains.

And when, after a fortnight
being seasick, there's the statue,
and buildings reaching up
to the sky. Streets full of people.
The clang of a bell, someone yelling

as you almost get run over.
More things happening every second
in New York, than Lutsk in a year.

Al lived on Kingston Avenue, Brooklyn,
all of his life, with the wife
his mother had picked out for him.
Beth never married. She was still waiting
for Mr. Right.

Of such is the Kingdom
of Heaven. Say that I sent you.

There You Are

The concierge climbed five flights
to complain. Erich was on the stairs,
just coming up. "Throw her down,
Vicki," he shouted, "I'll catch her!"

There were good times in Paris.
That was before the war,
of course, and La Rafle.

A girl came into the room.
She went over to Erich
and put an arm around him.
"I've done all my homework,
Papa. Can I go now?"

"Lisa is an American girl,"
he said. "Already she has boyfriends."

*

La Rafle. I looked it up.
A policeman comes to the door . . .
"Monsieur, you and Madame
and the children must be packed
and report yourselves to the stadium
tomorrow by seven o'clock."

So tomorrow, there you are.
And they walk you to the station
and give you to the Germans
with a list of names, and two fingers
to the cap. Signing off.

From there by train to Drancy.
Then Auschwitz, the last stop,
"letzer Termin," and the gas.

*

It's late, and I'm hurrying
to pack. I have to catch up.
The streets are full of bicycles
going to work. Then I'm running.

And then, with a sense of relief,
I see them up ahead.
There must be thousands moving
like a river through the street.

Some with big suitcases,
looking well dressed and well fed,
others as though they've been living
under a bridge for weeks.

I shout, "Where are you going?"
"To the station!" they shout back.

Viet-Cong

One moonlit night in Quinhon
they were standing at the window
when she grasped his arm. "Viet-Cong!"

By moonlight he sees them still,
in black pajamas flitting
like cats from roof to roof.

Remembering the Sixties

If I close my eyes I can hear
the voice of Mario Savio . . .
Aptheker, a voice like a corncrake,
and Weinberg: "Don't trust anyone
over thirty."

       Where's he now?
According to the *New York Times*,
on Wall Street, making money—
"innocently employed" as someone,
I think Doctor Johnson, said.

We marched for peace from Berkeley
to Oakland, carrying candles.
It was dark on the way back.
The candles went singly glimmering
down side streets, and went out.

The Believer

She comes once a week . . . and talks.
Her husband, Jim, is an invalid.
Up to six years ago
a healthy, goodlooking man,
now it exhausts him just to walk
from his chair to the dinner table.

He is irritable and shouts at her
then says that he's sorry.
The worst thing is, he expects her
to drop whatever she's doing
and bring something. He's watching TV
with the boys, and calls to her, "Eadie,
would you bring a glass of water."
He wouldn't think of asking the boys.

She takes her paraphernalia
to the bathroom: bucket and mop,
Tilex for the walls, Bon-Ami
for the bathtub and sink. Ammonia
for the toilet. Thirty minutes later
reenters and resumes.

"You ought to treat him," said her mother-in-law,
"with more consideration."
"What do you want me to do?"
she said. "Sit beside him and hold his hand,
and cry all day long?"

She belongs to the Church of the Redeemer
and believes she will be saved,
and that all the people she cares about
will be saved too. It stands to reason

if you're a believer, don't it?
And I have to agree, it does.

The Dental Assistant

She has a steady boyfriend . . .
he wants to get married,
she doesn't think they ought to yet.
(She tells me this while adjusting
the headrest, clipping a napkin
at the back of my neck.)

                Another thing,
he's a couch potato . . . sits for hours
switching from channel to channel.

Then Dr. Weiss comes in
and asks how are we today,
and that's the end of friendly conversation.
From here on, the sound of the tube
sucking, the whine of the drill . . .

I wonder if she and her boyfriend
will work out their differences.

Sex. It usually is.

The Walker on Main Street

He would be wearing an overcoat
no matter what the season,
a hat, a scarf and gloves.
The same on a hot day in July
as on the coldest winter day.

He appeared at the top of Main Street
and walked down it, swinging his arms,
speaking to no one. At the harbor,
right turn on Broadway. Right again
on East Main, past the antiques
and The Good Times. Right again
by the post office, and so back
out on Main Street, to 25A.

He came every day one summer,
to the astonishment of strangers.
If any of them asked . . . "Oh yes,"
we'd say, and go back to whatever
we were doing before they asked.
They were strangers, he was one of us.

He used to appear around noon.
One day the clocks showed twelve,
twelve-thirty, and still no sign.
At one o'clock, J. K. Ashby Junior
came out and stood on the sidewalk.
He was joined by Pete from Moore's Market
and Judy from Her Ideas.

They looked the street up and down,
they looked at one another,
shook their heads, and went back in.

He has never been seen since.
But sometimes, after a good dinner
when people start to reminisce,
the man in the overcoat comes walking
quickly, speaking to no one,
always in the same direction
for a reason only known to him.

Stairs

He talked about his son.
Tom had never been sick in his life. . . .
One day, up at the college,
he climbed five flights of stairs
and suddenly collapsed and died.
It seems that one side of the heart
was much larger than the other.

Stairs, he said as he measured . . .
When you build them you have to be sure
they're exactly the same height,
for when you step up or down
"the eye makes an adjustment."
If one is slightly higher or lower
you'll stumble.

He stands in the muddy area
where the stairs will be, writing numbers
with a pencil on the wall.
We'll have a devil of a time later
getting them off with soap and water.
But we forgive him. He is a man
with a great deal on his mind.

Working Out

A middleaged man named Doherty
had the locker next to mine.
A detective. He showed me
scar tissue near his heart
where a bullet had gone in.

A new member joined, a woman
who was doing physiotherapy.
She was beautiful to watch
at Leg Curl and Leg Extension,
straddling a bench or lying down.

The tone of the whole place changed.
When she came, Doherty would run over
and be solicitous:
how was she feeling today,
and she mustn't overdo it.

Then she no longer came, she was cured,
and everything reverted:
the young men blowdrying their hair
assiduously, the old
telling their dirty stories.

And Doherty working out
at Pullover, Double Chest,
and Torso Arm . . . lifting weights
as though it were he or they
in a struggle to the death.

The Indian Student

I said, "I can't talk to you
this morning, I'm very busy."
He jumped back two paces,
and smiled and said, "You have
a very pleasant irascibility."

I said, "Come to my house
on Saturday. You can tell me
everything on your mind, all at once."

So there we were, in my study,
with his father, the Sanskrit scholar
who died at twenty-three,
the uncle who kept a "dramshop,"
another uncle who was poisoned,
and a cousin named Maya. . . .

"Stop!" I said. "Go back
to the uncle who was poisoned."
"Yes," he said, "by his mistress."

He spoke in a monotone
of the village where he grew up
and, when he was a man, in Calcutta,
sharing a room above the market . . .
a shuffling all night long
going by, a murmur of voices.

*

A book came in the mail, from India:
cardboard covers and cheap paper,
Wings of Song by Sastri,
dedicated to his "friend and mentor."

In India when someone chooses you
as his mentor, from then on
you're in his debt, obliged
to help him . . . find him a job.
When he marries you're expected
to help support his family.

There's no end to it . . . the quarreling
next door. The sound of a flute,
and a murmur and shuffling.

All those people in the street
who stay up all night long.

Old Field Stories

He is querulous and constipated,
Whitman tells us, but he still writes
a song every day of his life.

There is plenty to write about
in Old Field where we live.
Last night the constable phoned
the animal warden. "There's a rabbit,"
he said, "that's acting strange."

It was moving very slow.
Then she saw a pair of eyes
up the road, the fox.
It must have chased the rabbit
and tired it out.

As I said, lots of stories,
and some strange ones. But few occasions
for song, as far as I know.

August

Gulls float on the Sound,
geese and ducks swim close to shore,
the reeds are growing tall in August.

As you round Cannon Bluff
the harbor spreads before you:
the ferry to Connecticut
either coming in or going out;
restaurants, fast-food places
and boutiques for the summer crowd.
The hospital, St. Anne's, large and yellow
on a hill to the west, looking down.
On the other side, to the east,
the Islandwide Lighting Company:
three chimneys like three sisters,
two of them tall and slender,
the third one short and stout.

There is everything you could want
on Main Street: a Chemical Bank,
drugstore, furniture store, newsagent.
A woman arranging dresses
in the window of Dillman's.
A man unloading cases of beer
from a truck. A woman passes . . .
he watches her as she walks away.

So it goes, day by day,
except when there's a traffic accident.
Or when a woman from Smithtown
and another from Miller Place
are arrested for petty larceny; when unknown
assailants throw a rock
through the rear sliding glass door

of a home on East Meadow Road;
when vandals tear up sods and dump garbage
on the twelfth green of the Oakwood Golf Course.

Then there will be an editorial
in *Suffolk News* on the rise of crime,
and Reverend Hunt will deliver his sermon,
"Watchman, what of the night?"
(There were incidents of vandalism
in Palestine long ago.)

But most of the time most people
lead decent, productive lives.
And there's plenty to see and do
on the calendar of events:
the North Shore Pro Musica
at the First Presbyterian Church;
a Pottery Demonstration;
a Two Day Conference on Exporting.

*

There was a wind coming in gusts
from the sea, humid and warm,
and the hand ceased from typing,
the mower from mowing his lawn.

It was raining when night came,
and the wind still rising. Branches
tossed, and the leaves were rushing,
tormented, this way and that.
There was a sound high in the air
like the passing of an express train.
A tree fell with a tearing sound
and crack, and the lights went out.

We sat in the dark with a candle
and listened to the wind,

and thought of those who were lying
in endless night, forgotten
as though they had never been.
And the wind said, Be afraid
and know yourselves.

                    So saying,
the great wind turned outward,
and with a distant rumbling
as of boxcars being moved,
returned to the sea where it came.

Her Weekend in the Country

My wife's sister is visiting
for the weekend. Never again!

She can hardly wait to be back
in her apartment in Sutton Place . . .

East 56th Street,
a walk to the United Nations.

She's bored with the chatter
about people she doesn't know . . .

old copies of *The New Yorker*,
the glassed-in porch with a view

of snowflakes lightly falling
on grass and a child's swing.

Patsy

When the Whip is still and the Ferris wheel
hangs in the air unmoving,

and PRINCESS MY-IMMBA & Her Very Talented
& Versatile Baboons are asleep,

and so is Johnny the hell driver
THE THRILL OF A LIFETIME

HELL DRIVING with a Dodge Pick-Up Truck
hurtling 70 feet through space . . .

then her voice calls from a mountain
on the wind like a widow ghost,

crazy for feeling so lonely
and crazy for loving you.

Honeymoon

Uncle Bob prayed over the groom:
"Let him establish Kingdom principles."
Aunt Shirley prayed for the bride:
"Father, I pray an anointing on her."
"Love," said Reverend Philips,

"is insensitive, love is invalueless."
He said that we merger together
in holy matrimony,
and the choir burst into song:
"He waits for us, and waits for us."

        *

Every day they went swimming in the pool
and rode the two water scooters.
They rented two deck chairs
and sat on the sand in the sun.
A breeze made the palm leaves whisper.

The sea is green close to shore,
further out it is blue.
The ship standing still on the horizon
makes you think of sailing away
forever with the one you love.

        *

Jennifer ordered the roast beef platter.
Mike had the fish cakes.
"I thought you didn't like fish,"
she said. "Well," he said, "I guess you were wrong."
Tears came to her eyes. The honeymoon was over.

But then they went to their room
and everything was OK.
In the evening they went dancing
and stayed up late on the veranda
looking at the lights and the moon.

*

And you, *hypocrite lecteur,*
what makes you so superior?

An Academic Story

One day during his office hour
a young woman appeared. "I'm Merridy,"
she said, "Merridy Johnson.
I'd like you to read my poems."

He said that he didn't teach writing.
"But couldn't you just look
and tell me, are they any good?"

She was carrying a flat white box.
She removed some tissue paper,
lifted out an album with a red cover,
and handed it to him carefully.

The poems were written in green ink
with flowers and birds in the margins.

She said, "What do you think?"
He said there were some nice images.
"Where?" she said, and leaned to see.

                    *

His wife didn't go to poetry readings.
He went by himself and sat at the rear.

But this evening he stayed to the end
and went to the reception afterwards
at Professor "Pat" Melrose's house.

When he arrived the poet was reciting
again, to a circle on the floor.
Merridy patted a place beside her
and he sat.

Her eyes were shining.
Poetry gave her goosebumps.
Taking his hand she showed him where.

Melrose was a poet himself.
And there was nothing professorial
about these evenings. They were . . . bohemian.

Melrose's wife, a little woman
with a face like a rhesus monkey's
went around the room winking and grimacing.
"The pot's in the kitchen, acid's in the study"
she said with an eldritch laugh.

*

He was stoned, and so was she,
going down Spruce Street
with a moon in the redwoods
and San Francisco glittering
on the bay, through the fog.

The poetry was great, she thought.
"As great as Bob Dylan's?"
But irony was wasted on her,
she was innocent. Like her room
with its posters of Joan Baez
and, right on, Bob Dylan.

Her books . . . *Siddhartha,* Ferlinghetti,
Alan Watts and Suzuki on Zen.
They spoke for her generation
like the *Poems, Sacred and Moral*
of a mid-Victorian girl.

And as softly as saying her prayers
she murmured, "Let's go to bed."

*

Sam Mendelson was a font of wisdom.
He knew there was going to be an opening
for a medievalist at Ohio,
and who was sleeping with whom.
He said, "But they don't do it here.
They go to San Francisco."

The MLA was meeting in San Francisco.
There were sessions he had to go to,
Henry told his wife, Cynthia,
all very boring but unavoidable.
He'd be back in three days.

He and Merridy walked all over.
They ate at Fisherman's Wharf
and rode on a trolley.
They explored Chinatown,
and went dancing at Whisky a Go-Go.
He took her to The Hungry I
and they saw *Doctor Zhivago*.

*

"Cynthia," he said, "I'm home!"
No answer. He went upstairs,
unpacked his suitcase, came down,
and was settling in with a scotch
in front of *The Untouchables*
when he had what he could only describe
as a sinking feeling.

He took the stairs two at a time.
No, her dresses were in the closet,
her doodads still on the table.

She came through the door
minutes later. She'd been shopping.
"How was the MLA?"

He gave her a circumstantial account
of the sessions he'd attended
in Yeats and Pound and Eliot.

"I had a vision," she said.
"I saw you in a room with a woman
as clearly as you're sitting here."

And he had always thought of her
as a person of limited imagination!

                    *

He was up for promotion, to associate
with tenure.

            "Melrose is out to get you,"
Sam said. "Can you think of a reason?"

Henry thought. He shook his head.

"Did you insult Mrs. Melrose?"

"I don't recall. I may have."

At the meeting to decide his fate—
they're supposed to be confidential
but someone always tells—
Melrose spoke.

            His only concern
was in the area of collegiality.

"Associate" . . . think what that means.
Someone you have to your house,
introduce to your wife . . .

If the fathers and mothers of the children
to whom we stand *in loco parentis*
were here, they would ask, they would demand to know,
not is he supposed to be clever
and did the *New York Times* or some other publication
give a book a good review,
but is he a moral man?

Henry wasn't promoted and he didn't get tenure.

        *

That was why he was at the MLA.
He was being interviewed at five
by a man from upstate New York.
They had a place for a lost soul
somewhere in the Finger Lakes,
teaching rhetoric.

        "I've never taught it,
but I don't suppose it matters.
I've been speaking it all my life."
He laughed nervously. "Shall we have another?"

But I had to go. We were interviewing
on the fourteenth floor.

        "You're just in time,"
said the Chair. "Mrs. Harris
is going to tell us about her dissertation
on women's writing."

        "Ms Harris,"

she said. "The title is *Theory
and Praxis in Feminist Criticism*."
In a little while it became obvious
we weren't interviewing her, she was interviewing us.

We used to teach poetry, now it's theory.
There's no longer room in the system
for a mind as romantic as Henry's.

After a Light Snowfall

On a day when snow has fallen
lightly, sprinkling the ground,
and a flock of small birds
are hopping and flying about,
a poem returns to haunt me.

"As you have wasted your life here in this place
You have wasted it in every part of the world."

I am disturbed by the words
of a man I never knew, who lived
in a country I have never visited.
How is it he knows about me,
and that I have not lived
for the good of others, putting their needs
before my own? That I have not been
a perfect husband and father.
That I have not written a book
that graces every other coffee table,
or made a discovery or invention
that will save lives and relieve human suffering?

How can he say I have wasted my life?
What can he possibly know about me?
And yet I see that he does.

Shoo-Fly Pie

The plain-faced Mennonite woman
with her little white cap
selling cheese and shoo-fly pie . . .

Existence can be so peaceful—
you only have to be good.
What am I doing here?

Like a Glass of Tea

"Life," said Joe Butensky,
"is like a glass of tea."
If you asked him why,
"How do I know?" he would say.
"Am I a philosopher?"

I was reminded of Joe
the other day on the subway.
Sitting across from me
was a woman wearing a jacket
with the 82nd Airborne patch,
pants of glistening spandex,
and running shoes. Two wires
hung from her head to the stereo
she was holding in her lap.

I thought of Joe. Don't ask me
why. Am I a philosopher?

A Clearing

I had come to Australia
for ten weeks, as a guest of the state.
My duties were light: to confer
with students. They didn't want to—
they came once or twice, that was all.

One night someone knocked: a student
with some poems she'd like me to see.
The next day I observed her
in the dining room, and went over.
"I liked" I began to say . . .
She lifted her hands, imploring me
not to speak. All around her
they were talking about the usual subjects,
motorbikes and football.
If it got around that she wrote poems . . .

At night I would sit in my room
reading, keeping a journal,
and, with the aid of a map,
trying to learn the positions
of the southern constellations.
I'd look at them on the map,
then go outside and try to find them
in the sky before I forgot.

I had recently been divorced
and was starting a new life,
as they say. The world lies before you,
where to live and what to be.
A fireman? An explorer?
An astronaut? Then you look in the mirror.
It was night sweats. Listening
to an echo of the end.

Roger had a live-in girlfriend.
They asked if I'd like to go with them
to a party and sleep over.

He drove. I looked at the gum trees.
Not the Outback, but country . . .
cattle and kangaroos,
and flies, getting in your eyes,
ears, nose, and mouth.
Once, talking to a sheepherder,
I watched a fly crawl over his face
from his eye to his mouth,
and start walking back
before he brushed it off.
They learn to put up with nature
and not make a fuss like us.

We arrived. I was introduced,
and they made up a bed for me
on the porch at the back.
Then the party began to arrive:
Australians, lean and athletic.
They put a tape on the stereo,
turned it up full blast,
and danced, or stood and shouted
to each other above to noise.

I danced with two or three women
and tried shouting. Then I went
and sat on the bed on the porch.
There was nowhere to go, no door
I could close to shut out the noise.

*

So I went for a walk
in the dark, away from the sound.
There were gum trees, wind rustling
the leaves. Or was it snakes?

There are several venomous kinds.
The taipan. There's a story
about a child who was sitting
on a log and fell backward
onto a taipan. It struck him
twenty-three times.
There's the tiger snake and the brown.
When they have finished telling you
about snakes, they start on spiders.

You don't need these—you have only to walk
into the bush. There are stories
about campers who did, and were lost
and never seen again.

All this was on my mind.
I stepped carefully, keeping the lights
of the house behind me in sight.
And when I saw a clearing
in the trees, I walked to it.

*

I stood in the middle of the clearing
looking at the sky. It was glittering
with unknown constellations.
Everything I had ever known
seemed to have disappeared.
And who was I, standing there
in the middle of Australia
at night? I had ceased to exist.
There was only whatever it was

that was looking at the sky
and listening to the wind.

After a while I broke away
and went back to the lights and the party.
A month later I left Australia.

But ever since, to this day,
there has been a place in my mind,
a clearing in the shadows,
and above it, stars and constellations
so bright and thick they seem to rustle.
And beyond them . . . infinite space,
eternity, you name it.

There's nothing that stands between me
and it, whatever it is.

Index of Titles

Acknowledgments

The American Poetry Review: "The Appointment," "Confessions of a Professor of English," "Footnotes to Fodor's *Spain*," "Kaimana Beach," "A Letter from Beazil," "The Listeners," "The Long Afternoon";

Atlanta Review: "In the Alpha Cradle";

The Cortland Review: "A Farewell to His Muse";

Critical Quarterly: "Grand Forks";

Five Points: "Driving," "The Fence," "The Floor Lamp," "Homeless Men," "Peter's Dream," "Wash, Dry, and Fold," "The *Wow!* Factor";

Harvard Review: "Reading the Times," "Variations on a Theme by Shostakovich";

The Hudson Review: "All Sorts of Things," "The Blue Coast," "The Children's Choir," "Country Doctor," "Foursome," "'He's asleep'," "In Country Houses," "Inspiration," "Nero in Love," "Sanctuary Road" as "Out on the Island," "A Shearling Coat," "A Walk with Bashō";

Image: "Lilies of the Field" as "The Sparrow and the Lily";

Janus: "Any Time Now";

Princeton University Library Chronicle: "A Wandering Life";

The New Criterion: "The Owner of the House";

River Styx: "Graduation," "An Orchid";

Visions: "At Journey's End."

The author thanks Mr. Robert McDowell and Story Line Press for permission to reprint poems from *There You Are*. And thanks Mr. Tom Radko and Wesleyan University Press for permission to reprint poems from *A Dream of Governors*.

About the Author

Educated at Munro College (Jamaica, West Indies) and at Columbia, where he received his doctorate, Louis Simpson has taught at Columbia, the University of California at Berkeley, and at the State University of New York at Stony Brook. The author of seventeen books of poetry, he has received the Rome Fellowship of the American Academy of Arts and Letters, a *Hudson Review* Fellowship, Guggenheim Foundation fellowships, and the Pulitzer Prize. He lives in Stony Brook, New York.

BOA Editions, Ltd.

AMERICAN POETS CONTINUUM SERIES

Colophon

The Owner of the House: New Collected Poems 1940–2001
by Louis Simpson
was set with Adobe Garamond fonts and Woodtype Ornaments
by Richard Foerster, York Beach, Maine.
The cover was designed by Daphne Poulin-Stofer
with art by Don Resnick.
Manufacturing was by McNaughton & Gunn, Saline, Michigan.

•

Special support for this book came from the following individuals:

Rachel Berghash
Deborah Smith-Bernstein & Martin B. Bernstein
Judith Bishop
Nancy & Alan Cameros
Susan De Witt Davie
Debra Kang Dean & Bradley P. Dean
Peter & Suzanne Durant
Arlene Eager • Hon. Sandra L. Frankel
Dr. Henry & Beverly French
Robert & Adele Gardner
Kip & Deb Hale
Peter & Robin Hursh • Robert & Willy Hursh
Richard Garth & Mimi Hwang
Archie & Pat Kutz
Boo Poulin
Samuel Post • Deborah Ronnen
Andrea & Paul Rubery
Elaine Schwager
Sue Stewart
Memye Curtis Tucker
Thomas R. Ward • Michael Waters
Pat & Michael Wilder
Mark Williams

✳